CGI & PERL

in easy steps

MIKE MCGRATH

COMPUTER STEP

In easy steps is an imprint of Computer Step
Southfield Road . Southam
Warwickshire CV47 OFB . England

http://www.ineasysteps.com

Notice of Liability

Every effort has been made to ensure that this book contains accurate
and current information. However, Computer Step and the author shall
not be liable for any loss or damage suffered by readers as a result of
any information contained herein.

Trademarks

All trademarks are acknowledged as belonging to their respective
companies.

Printed and bound in the United Kingdom

ISBN 1-84078-027-4

Table Of Contents

Using Arrays   59

5

Using Hashes   73

6

Subroutines   81

7

Perl Functions   89

8

Pattern Matching   101

9

CGI From Web Pages   115

10

Working With Files   131

11

Perl Tools & Environment

Welcome to the world of CGI & Perl. This initial chapter shows how to download and install the free Perl interpreter that is needed to run Perl scripts. The benefits and features of a purpose-built Perl editor are demonstrated. Also there is a guide to download and install the free Xitami web server to create a local CGI intranet environment.

Covers

Chapter One

Perl Interpreter

The convention used for the way paths are stated throughout this book is as follows:

Windows continues the DOS format that uses back slashes in path addresses such as C:\Perl\bin\perl. The same path address uses forward slashes in the Hypertext Transfer Protocol (HTTP) so is referred to as C:/Perl/bin/perl. Consequently any references to paths in the general text normally uses the Windows format whereas paths stated in Perl code examples follow the HTTP format.

The Common Gateway Interface (CGI) is the standard used to pass information between a web server and a browser.

CGI allows the browser to communicate with server-side programs written in any programming language.

The Practical Extraction and Reporting Language (Perl) is most commonly used for this purpose.

The Perl language was originally created in 1986 by a programmer named Larry Wall in order to perform specific data-handling tasks within the company where he worked.

Since then Perl has become freely available and has been greatly extended by contributions from around the world.

This book is an introduction to Perl programming that will demonstrate by example how to write Perl scripts that can interact with a web browser via the internet or an intranet.

These examples will illustrate both how Perl scripts can dynamically create web page content and handle data sent from the web browser when it is received on the server.

Perl programs are written in plain text and are normally used in that form without compilation into byte code.

Instead the Perl programs, or "scripts", are loaded directly onto the server and are run by the Perl interpreter.

For more on client-side JavaScript programming please refer to "JavaScript in easy steps" at http://www.ineasysteps.com

This is similar to the way that client-side JavaScripts are run in the major web browsers using the JavaScript interpreter built-in to their software.

When the browser encounters JavaScript code in a web page its JavaScript interpreter is called to read the script and execute the instructions that it contains.

PC operating systems do not normally contain a Perl interpreter so this will need to be installed before running any Perl scripts on a local system.

In order to try the examples in this book the Perl interpreter should be installed first.

Installing Perl

The Perl interpreter is available at http://www.perl.com as a free download in versions to suit several operating systems.

Perl for Microsoft Windows needs the Win32 binary version.

Older versions of Windows 95 may also need to add the runtime file msvcrt.dll to the Windows/System folder from the Microsoft website. This file is included as standard with later versions of Windows.

For Perl installations with older versions of Windows it may be necessary to download support for the Microsoft Installer (MSI) format before Perl can be installed.

MSI 1.1 is freely available from the Microsoft web site at http://www.microsoft.com as a file named InstMsi.exe.

Running the Perl installer produces a Custom Setup dialog box where installation components can be selected and a location specified at which Perl will be installed.

It is advisable to accept the default location of C:\Perl\.

The extensive examples and documentation supplied with the Perl interpreter need not be installed initially but can be added later by running the Perl installer again.

Before Perl is finally installed the Setup Options dialog box offers to make optional changes to Windows' environment.

It is important to select the option to add the location of Perl to the system's path so that Windows will know where to find the Perl interpreter when scripts are being run.

The Perl path at the default location could also be set by adding this line into the autoexec.bat file

SET PATH= C:\PERL\BIN;"%PATH%"; on Windows 95/98

ActivePerl Setup

Choose Setup Options

Choose the options that suit you best

☑ Add Perl to the PATH environment variable

☑ Create Perl file extension association

Perl Editor

Because Perl scripts are just plain text they can be written in any simple text editor such as Windows Notepad.

However, there are several specialized Perl editors available that offer significant benefits when developing Perl scripts.

Most Perl editors have a text window where the script code can be written and also an output window that will instantly display the output from that script.

So a specialized Perl editor enables a script to be written, run and amended quickly.

Also a Perl editor will normally highlight key words in a script to clarify the code during development.

In the event that the code contains an error the Perl editor's syntax checker can help to debug the code by pin-pointing the line and position where an error has occurred.

These and other labour-saving features make the creation of Perl scripts in a specialized Perl editor preferable to using a standard text editor.

There are many more Perl editors to try – search for "Perl editors" at http://www.download.com.

The Perl editor used throughout this book is the DzSoft Perl Editor available for download from http://www.dzsoft.com.

This is not free software but, at the of time writing, the freely available trial version is only restricted by a 6kb limit on the size of script that can be created.

To run scripts beyond this limit will require a registered version of the DzSoft Perl Editor.

All the examples depicted in this book will be less than the specified limit so they could run on this trial version.

The next few pages illustrate the Perl Editor interface and demonstrate the features mentioned above together with other useful features that are included.

Many of the Perl Editor features are used to demonstrate example script code given throughout this book.

Editor - Preview

The Perl Editor launches in normal editing mode where Perl script code can be written in the open window:

 The Perl Editor also has a button-style toolbar but that is not shown here in order to save space.

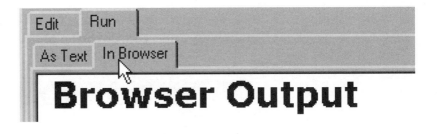

Clicking on the Run tab calls the Perl interpreter to process the contents of the Edit window. Two more tabs then appear to select the type of output display to be viewed.

When the "In Browser" tab is selected the output from the Perl script is displayed as it would appear in a web browser:

Selecting the "As Text" tab switches the window to reveal the Html source code behind the displayed web page, just like using View Source in a web browser:

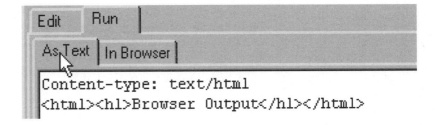

Editor - Syntax Checker

A feature of the Perl Editor that is unavailable in regular text editors is the ability to check Perl code for syntax errors.

Time spent searching for a missing bracket that is causing a script error can be eliminated – the Syntax Checker simply tells you the location in the script where the error occurs.

Whenever the Perl Editor runs a script the syntax is automatically checked for errors. The Syntax Checker can also be run from the Run menu or by pressing the F12 key.

The syntax checker can also display information about non-fatal errors if the Warnings feature is enabled in the Run dialog box.

If errors are found the Syntax Checker opens a Messages window to display information on each error:

> **Messages**
>
> syntax error
>   at C:\WINDOWS\TEMP\DzTemp.pl line 5, near "print"
> Can't find string terminator "DOC" anywhere before EOF
>   at C:\WINDOWS\TEMP\DzTemp.pl line 6.

Place the cursor over an error description in the Messages window then double-click to be taken to the exact line of code in the Edit window where that error occurs.

In some cases the Syntax Checker will even offer a possible solution such as "Missing semi-colon in previous line?".

Editor - Features

The Unix, Windows, and Macintosh operating systems use different characters to denote the end of a line in a text file.

Unix uses a linefeed(LF), Mac uses a carriage return (CR) and Windows uses both (CRLF).

As most web servers run a variety of Unix it is important to change the line-endings of Perl scripts that have been written on a Windows platform to avoid confusion by the server after the script has been uploaded.

Perl Editor has a simple option under the File menu to ensure that all file endings will use the Unix format:

Windows can interpret Unix line endings so set the option for line-endings permanently to Unix format.

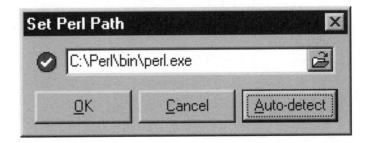

The Perl Editor should automatically detect the Perl interpreter but the location can also be specified manually using Set Perl Path under the Tools menu.

The Perl Editor has many other useful features to assist the easy creation of Perl scripts but this introduction has detailed those of greatest importance when starting out.

Xitami Web Server

In order to create a local CGI intranet environment the local system must first have a web server application.

The Xitami web server is ideal for testing CGI scripts on a Windows operating system.

Xitami is free, fast, and simply really good at its job. This is a professional web server that will run out of the box but lets you configure it in every possible way.

Download the latest production release of Xitami from the official web site at http://www.xitami.com.

The download is an executable file of less than 1mb in size.

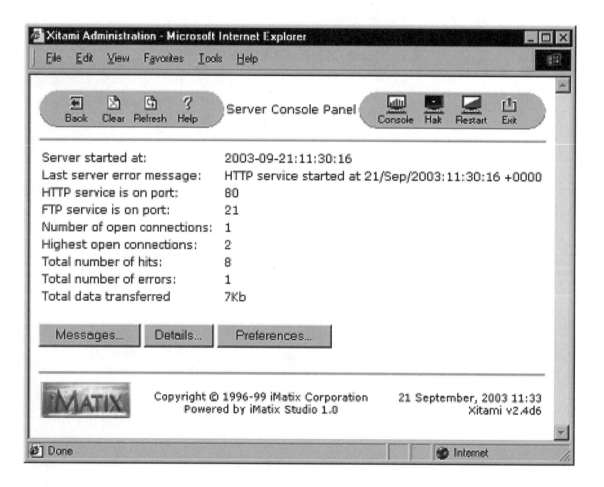

Installing Xitami

The Xitami installation is the simplest of any web browser.

Run the downloaded executable file to start the installation then accept the licence terms in the dialog box.

Now select the destination directory at C:\Xitami as shown:

 Xitami can be pronounced as "chee-ta-mee" or "ki-ta-mee".

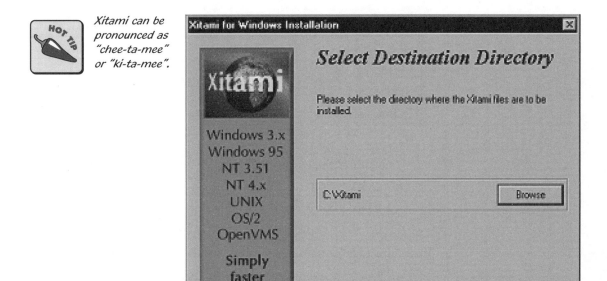

 Choose the option to manually start Xitami if this is preferable.

Specify a convenient start menu location for the Xitami icon then accept the default option to have the Xitami web server start automatically when Windows is loaded.

Next enter a memorable user name and password.

The user name and password will be required later to access the Xitami Administration area where the web server can be configured for different requirements.

Finally accept the default server profile as normal then click the "Next" button to complete the installation.

Xitami is now installed on the local hard drive at C:\Xitami

Local Host Environment

Installation of the Xitami web server creates a directory at the specified location of C:\Xitami.

There are many standard sub-directories contained within the Xitami main directory, as seen below:

Only two of these directories are immediately noteworthy.

The folder named "cgi-bin" is where all CGI scripts must be placed to be visible by the web server.

The folder named "webpages" is where all Html documents must be placed to be accessible by the server.

All the other folders merely hold incidental information.

The "localhost" domain name can be replaced with the given system local domain name or the default IP address of 127.0.0.1.

Start the Xitami web server if it is not already running.

To test the local intranet environment place a sample Html file, named "sample.htm", into the webpages folder .

Now open a web browser and address the sample page using the "localhost" domain for the local intranet.

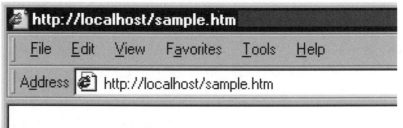

Getting Started

This chapter fully illustrates a first Perl script and introduces the three variable types that are used to store information. Syntax rules of the Perl language are discussed and data joining (concatenation) is demonstrated.

Covers

Chapter Two

Hello World Script

This initial script starts with the so-called "shebang" line whose name is derived from the line's first two characters "#" - sharp and "!" - bang.

The rest of the line states the local path to the Perl interpreter so that the script can be read, or "parsed".

All regular Perl scripts must start with the shebang line.

In the illustration the path "usr/bin/perl" is a typical Unix path whereas "c:/perl/bin/perl" might be a Windows path.

Whatever the path is to the Perl interpreter on the host system it must be inserted here and any ISP hosting CGI scripts will gladly confirm their correct path.

The Perl Editor allows any shebang line while using its' own Perl path. So code with a Unix shebang path can be written and tested on a Windows setup.

```
hello.cgi

File   Edit   Search   View   Run   Quick Insert   Tools

Edit  |  Run  |

1 #!/usr/bin/perl
2
3 print "Content-type:";
4 print "text/html\n\n";
5 print "<html>\n";
6 print "<h1>Hello World!</h1>\n";
7 print "</html>\n";
```

All Perl code statements must be terminated by a semi-colon.

All the other lines begin with a "print" and end with a ";". In Perl "print" means "output", so that the content contained within the quotes will be output by the script.

Because the script is creating html content the first outputs need to declare this with "Content type:text/html".

This is called the "MIME" type and is needed with all html output so that any browser receiving the output will expect to have html content rather than just plain text.

Hello World Output

The "\n" parts of the content is Perl syntax meaning start a new line and it is important that the mime type must always be on its own unique line.

Running this script produces text output formatted with the new line instructions as seen in the following illustration:

Always use a double new line after the mime type by adding "\n\n" to be sure it will be separated from the html code.

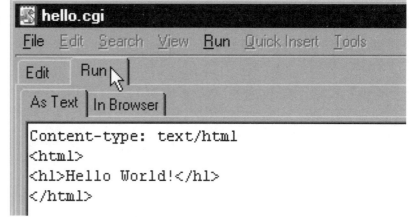

Viewing the output as text shows an html document in the same way that the source code of an html document may be viewed in a web browser.

Viewing the output as html displays the output in its desired form as it would normally be seen in a web browser:

Here Document

The multiple print statements in the previous example can be avoided by using a single "here document" statement.

A label is given to print using a "<<" syntax together with the label name enclosed in quotes and a terminating semi-colon. Now print will treat anything that follows as content until it encounters the given label.

The convention is to use only upper-case for labels in code.

It is important to note that the label following the content must be on a separate line with no other code and should not have quotes or a terminating semi-colon.

If other code were added to that line, or leading spaces, or if quotes or a semi-colon were added, the label would not be recognised and the script would produce an error.

In the example below the label is named as "DOC" then the content is all the code following the print statement until the label is next met.

The content need not be enclosed within quotes using this method nor are terminating semi-colons required other than the one to terminate the print statement.

The output remains identical to that on the previous page.

The content of "here document" may include quotes without any special consideration for syntax.

hellohere.cgi

File   Edit   Search   View   Run   Quick Insert   Tools

Edit | Run |

```perl
1  #!/usr/bin/perl
2
3  print <<"DOC";
4  Content-type: text/html\n\n
5  print <html>\n
6  print <h1>Hello World!</h1>\n
7  print </html>\n
8
9  DOC
```

Syntax Rules

A semi-colon must terminate each Perl statement in the same way that a period is used to terminate a sentence in the English language syntax rules.

Most importantly, Perl is a case-sensitive language where "var", "Var" and "VAR" are treated as three different words.

Spaces, tabs and new lines are collectively known as "whitespace" and are virtually ignored by Perl so the code may be formatted and indented to be more human-readable.

A comment line inside a "here document" will be treated as part of the string and will be output.

It is often useful to add comments to Perl code as explanation. The parser sees any text between "#" and the end of that line as a single-line comment, which it ignores.

Quotes within containing quotes should be escaped with a preceding backslash to prevent the text string terminating prematurely. Alternatively single quotes may be used inside containing double quotes as demonstrated in this example:

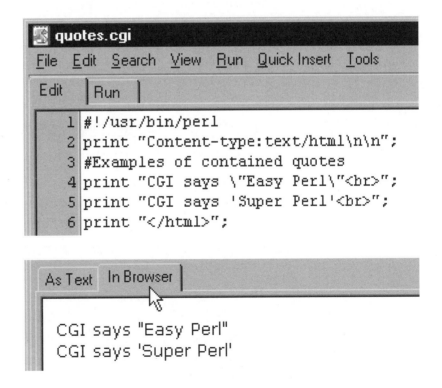

```
quotes.cgi
File  Edit  Search  View  Run  Quick Insert  Tools

Edit | Run |

1 #!/usr/bin/perl
2 print "Content-type:text/html\n\n";
3 #Examples of contained quotes
4 print "CGI says \"Easy Perl\"<br>";
5 print "CGI says 'Super Perl'<br>";
6 print "</html>";
```

```
As Text | In Browser |

CGI says "Easy Perl"
CGI says 'Super Perl'
```

Scalar Variables

A "variable" is simply a container in which a value may be stored for subsequent manipulation within a script.

Perl has three types of variable which each store data in slightly different ways but all three can store all types of data including integers, floating-point numbers and text strings.

The "scalar" variable is used to store a single item of data.

A scalar is created using a "$" followed by a given name that may comprise of any alphanumeric character, and optionally the underscore character, but must not begin with a number.

$var, $Var, $VAR and $_var123 are all valid variable names.

Avoid case problems by using only lower-case when choosing names in Perl scripts.

When naming variables it is advisable to be consistent in the use of case and also to choose meaningful variable names.

Data is assigned to the scalar using the "=" operator followed by the value to be stored and any text string values must be enclosed within quotes.

For example, $var = "Hello" declares a scalar variable named "var" with a string value of "Hello".

The variable can then be used anywhere in the script and its stored value will be substituted when the code runs.

So code to print "$var" would actually produce "Hello".

A scalar may also be assigned another scalar by reference.

The reference is actually the memory address at which the assigned variable is stored and is assigned by preceding the second variable name with a backslash.

For instance, $var2 = \$var1 assigns the address where the value held in $var1 is stored to the $var2 variable.

The value contained at the reference address can addressed in the script as ${$var2}. This is called "dereferencing".

The example on the facing page shows all these variables in action including reference assignation and dereferencing.

The "S" shape in the dollar sign is a reminder of the "S" in scalar to indicate that the type of variable is a scalar.

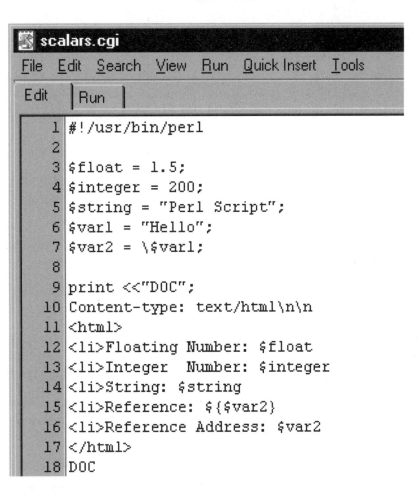

```perl
1  #!/usr/bin/perl
2
3  $float = 1.5;
4  $integer = 200;
5  $string = "Perl Script";
6  $var1 = "Hello";
7  $var2 = \$var1;
8
9  print <<"DOC";
10 Content-type: text/html\n\n
11 <html>
12 <li>Floating Number: $float
13 <li>Integer  Number: $integer
14 <li>String: $string
15 <li>Reference: ${$var2}
16 <li>Reference Address: $var2
17 </html>
18 DOC
```

A variable that contains a reference only produces an address unless it is first dereferenced.

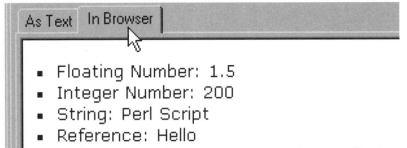

As Text | In Browser

- Floating Number: 1.5
- Integer Number: 200
- String: Perl Script
- Reference: Hello
- Reference Address: SCALAR(0xbb5f38)

Array Variables

The "array" variable is the second of the three types of Perl variable that can be used to store data.

The array variable is used to store multiple items of data.

Data is stored in the array variable as a list of items separated by commas. This is known as a "comma-delimited" list.

Each of the items in the list is called an array "element".

The list of elements is indexed so that each element can be addressed using its array index number.

Array indexing starts at zero so the first element is index number 0, the second element is index number 1, and so on.

An array is created using a "@" followed by a given name using the same naming conventions that apply to scalar variable names.

Data can be assigned to the array using the "=" operator followed by a pair of brackets containing the comma-delimited list of data that will form the array elements.

The element list may contain a mixture of integers, floating-point numbers and strings but any text string values must be enclosed within quotes.

See Chapter 5 for much more on arrays and how they may be used.

A single element in an array may be addressed using the "$" character followed by the array name then the index number of the required element enclosed within square brackets.

For example, with an array named @arr the first element would be addressed using the syntax $arr[0].

It may initially seem odd to address an array with a "$" but it may help to remember that "@" denotes a multiple list whereas "$" denotes a single item.

Assigning the array to a scalar variable will assign an integer value of the array's length.

The example on the facing page shows arrays in action.

The "a" shape in the @ symbol is a reminder of the "A" in array to indicate that the type of variable is an array.

```perl
1  #!/usr/bin/perl
2
3  @arr=("zero", 1, "TWO", 3.142, 4444);
4
5  $arrlength = @arr;
6
7  print <<"DOC";
8  Content-type: text/html\n\n
9  <html>
10 <li>List is @arr
11 <li>Element 0 is $arr[0]
12 <li>Element 1 is $arr[1]
13 <li>Element 2 is $arr[2]
14 <li>Element 3 is $arr[3]
15 <li>Element 4 is $arr[4]
16 <li>Length is $arrlength elements
17 </html>
18 DOC
```

Note that when outputting an array list such as "print @arr" the commas will be replaced by spaces.

As Text | **In Browser**

- List is zero 1 TWO 3.142 4444
- Element 0 is zero
- Element 1 is 1
- Element 2 is TWO
- Element 3 is 3.142
- Element 4 is 4444
- Length is 5 elements

Hash Variables

The "hash" variable is the third of the three types of Perl variable that can be used to store data.

The hash variable is used to store multiple items of data like the array variable but with one important difference.

Data is stored in the hash variable in a comma-delimited list that must have an even number of items.

This list forms an "associative array" that associates the first item with the second item, the third item with the fourth item, and so on.

See Chapter 6 for much more on hashes and how they may be used.

With these pairs the left-hand item is known as the "key" and the associated right-hand item is called the "value".

The value of any pair in a hash can be addressed in script using its associated key.

A hash is created using a "%" followed by a given name using the same naming conventions that apply to scalar variable names.

Data can be assigned to the hash using the "=" operator followed by a pair of brackets containing the comma-delimited list of data that will form the hash pairs.

The hash pairs list may contain a mixture of integers, floating-point numbers and strings but any text string values must be enclosed within quotes.

A single value in a hash may be addressed using the "$" character followed by the hash name then the name of the associated key element enclosed within curly brackets.

For example, with a hash named %data containing a pair with a key of "Colour" and its associated value of "Red" the value can be addressed using the syntax $data{"Colour"}.

This syntax uses a "$" because it is addressing a single item.

The example on the facing page shows a hash in action and illustrates how keys get associated values from the hash list.

...cont'd

The two "o" characters in the "%" symbol is a reminder of the pairs in any hash to indicate that the type of variable is a hash.

```
hashes.cgi
File  Edit  Search  View  Run  Quick Insert  Tools
Edit  |  Run

 1 #!/usr/bin/perl
 2
 3 %data=("int",100, "flt",3.142,
 4 "str","Hello", "Colour","Red",
 5 "gem","Diamond", 100,"One Hundred");
 6
 7 print <<"DOC";
 8 Content-type: text/html\n\n
 9 <html>
10 <li>Integer is $data{"int"}
11 <li>Floating Point is $data{"flt"}
12 <li>String is $data{"str"}
13 <li>Colour is $data{"Colour"}
14 <li>Gem is $data{"gem"}
15 <li>Score is $data{100}
16 </html>
17
18 DOC
```

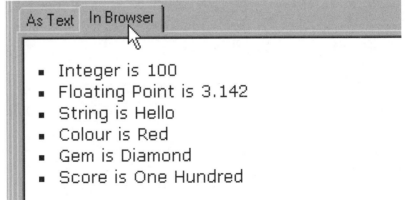

As Text | In Browser

- Integer is 100
- Floating Point is 3.142
- String is Hello
- Colour is Red
- Gem is Diamond
- Score is One Hundred

Concatenation

Variable values can be joined together, or "concatenated", in order to assign the concatenated value to another variable.

The "." period operator is placed between the variables, without any spaces, to concatenate their values.

For example, the statement $concat=$str1.$str2 assigns the concatenated value of $str1 and $str2 to the $concat variable.

Also $concat=$concat.$str1 would concatenate the existing value in the $concat variable with the value in $str1.

Concatenated variables still maintain their original values.

This statement can be better expressed in its shortened form of $concat.= $str1 as illustrated in the example below:

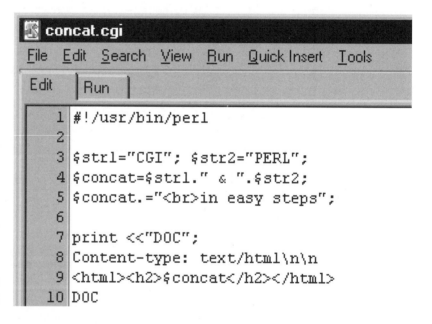

```
 1  #!/usr/bin/perl
 2
 3  $str1="CGI"; $str2="PERL";
 4  $concat=$str1." & ".$str2;
 5  $concat.="<br>in easy steps";
 6
 7  print <<"DOC";
 8  Content-type: text/html\n\n
 9  <html><h2>$concat</h2></html>
10  DOC
```

On line #4 the concatenation also adds a space so that the final string will appear correctly spaced.

As Text | In Browser

CGI & PERL
in easy steps

Performing Operations

This chapter demonstrates by example the many ways how Perl operators can manipulate script values.

Covers

Chapter Three

Arithmetic Operators

The arithmetical operators commonly used in Perl are listed in the table below along with the operations they perform:

Operator	Operation
+	Addition
-	Subtraction
*	Multiplication
**	Exponential Power
/	Division
%	Modulus
++	Increment
- -	Decrement

Mostly the arithmetic operators are straightforward but some are worthy of further explanation.

Using the power operator ** returns the value of the first operand raised by the power of the second so that 3**2=9.

The modulus operator will divide the first operand by the second operand and return the remainder of the operation. This is useful to determine odd or even numeric values.

Pre-increment operators (before the operand) can be seen in the loop example on page 51.

The increment + + and decrement -- operators alter the given value by 1. They may be placed before the operand to immediately return the new value. Alternatively they may be placed after the operand to firstly return the existing value before finally implementing the increase.

Care should be taken to bracket expressions where more than one operator is being used to clarify the operations:

```
a = b * c - d % e / f ;        # This is unclear
a = (b * c) - ((d % e) / f );  # This is clear
```

Arithmetical Operator Examples

Leave no spaces between the characters of the increment, decrement and power operators.

```perl
 1 #!/usr/bin/perl
 2
 3 $add = 20 + 30;
 4 $sub = 35.75 - 28.25;
 5 $mul = 8 * 50;
 6 $pow = 2 ** 5;
 7 $mod = 65 % 2;
 8 $inc = 5; $inc++;
 9 $dec = 5; $dec--;
10
11 print <<"DOC";
12 content-type: text/html\n\n
13 <html>
14 Addition is $add <BR>
15 Subtraction is $sub <BR>
16 Multiplication is $mul <BR>
17 Power is $pow <BR>
18 Modulus is $mod <BR>
19 Increment is $inc <BR>
20 Decrement is $dec <BR>
21 </html>
22 DOC
```

As Text | **In Browser**

Addition is 50
Subtraction is 7.5
Multiplication is 400
Power is 32
Modulus is 1
Increment is 6
Decrement is 4

Assignment Operators

The operators that are commonly used in Perl to assign values are all listed in the table below. All except the simple assign operator "=" are a shorthand form of a longer expression so each equivalent is also given for clarity.

Operator	Example	Equivalent
=	a = b	a = b
+=	a += b	a = a + b
-=	a -= b	a = a - b
*=	a *= b	a = a * b
/=	a /= b	a = a / b
%=	a %= b	a = a % b

The equality operator compares numeric values – see page 36.

It is important to regard the "=" operator as meaning "assign" rather than "equals" to avoid confusion with the equality operator "==".

With the example in the table the variable named "a" is assigned the value that is contained in the variable named "b" to become its new value.

The "+=" operator is most useful and has been used in earlier examples to add a second string to an existing string. In the table example the "+=" operator adds the value contained in variable "a" to the value contained in the variable named "b" then assigns the result to become the new value contained in variable "a".

All the other operators in the table work in the same way by making the arithmetical operation between the two values first, then assigning the result to the first variable to become its new value.

Assignment Operator Examples

```
Edit    Run

 1  #!/usr/bin/perl
 2
 3  $str = "Assignments With Perl";
 4  $num = 5;
 5  $add = 8; $add += $num;
 6  $sub = 8; $sub -= $num;
 7  $mul = 8; $mul *= $num;
 8  $div = 8; $div /= $num;
 9  $mod = 8; $mod = $mod % $num;
10
11  print <<"DOC";
12  content-type:text/html\n\n
13  <html>
14  <b>$str</b>
15  <li>Addition is $add
16  <li>Subtraction is $sub
17  <li>Multiplication is $mul
18  <li>Division is $div
19  <li>Modulus is $mod
20  </html>
21  DOC
```

```
As Text    In Browser

Assignments With Perl
  ▪ Addition is 13
  ▪ Subtraction is 3
  ▪ Multiplication is 40
  ▪ Division is 1.6
  ▪ Modulus is 3
```

Logical Operators

The three logical operators that can be used in Perl are listed in the table below:

Operator	Operation
&&	Logical AND
||	Logical OR
!	Logical NOT

The logical operators are used with operands that have the boolean values of true or false, or are values that can convert to true or false.

The logical "&&" operator will evaluate two operands and return true only if both operands themselves are true. Otherwise the "&&" operator will return false.

This is typically used in "conditional branching" where the direction of a Perl script is determined by testing two conditions. If both conditions are satisfied the script will go in a certain direction otherwise the script will take a different direction.

Unlike the "&&" operator that needs both operands to be true the "||" operator will evaluate its two operands and return true if either one of the operands itself returns true. If neither operand returns true then "||" will return false. This is useful in a Perl script to perform a certain action if either one of two test conditions has been met.

The third logical operator "!" is a unary operator that is used before a single operand. It returns the inverse value of the given operand so if the variable "a" had a value of true then "!a" would have a value of false. It is useful in Perl scripting to toggle the value of a variable in successive loop iterations with a statement like "a=!a". This will ensure that on each pass the value is changed, like flicking a light switch on and off.

Logical Operator Examples

Edit | Run

```perl
 1 #!/usr/bin/perl
 2
 3 $a = 0;  $b = 1;
 4 $a_inv = !$a;
 5 $both1 = ( $a && $a );
 6 $both2 = ( $a && $b );
 7 $both3 = ( $b && $b );
 8 $any1 = ( $a || $a );
 9 $any2 = ( $a || $b  );
10 $any3 = ( $b || $b );
11
12 print <<"DOC";
13 content-type: text/html\n\n
14 <html>
15 <b>AND</b>
16 a&amp;&amp;a=$both1
17 a&amp;&amp;b=$both2
18 b&amp;&amp;b=$both3 <br>
19 <b>OR</b>
20 a||a=$any1
21 a||b=$any2
22 b||b=$any3  <br>
23 <b>INVERT</b> a=$a !a=$a_inv
24 </html>
25 DOC
```

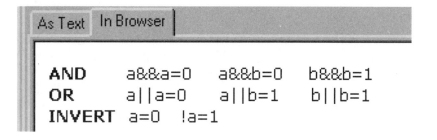

The boolean values of true and false are represented by the numeric values of 0 and 1.

As Text | In Browser

AND   a&&a=0   a&&b=0   b&&b=1
OR   a||a=0   a||b=1   b||b=1
INVERT a=0   !a=1

Numeric Comparison

The operators that are commonly used in Perl to compare two values are all listed in the table below:

Operator	Comparative Test
==	Equality – both sides are equal
!=	Inequality – both sides are not equal
<=>	Return result of left to right value comparison
>	Greater than – left side is greater than the right
<	Less than – left side is less than the right
>=	Greater than or equal to
<=	Less than or equal to

Equality and inequality operators are useful for testing the state of two variables to determine which direction the script should then branch.

The equality operator "==" compares two operands and will return true if both are equal in value.

Conversely the "!=" operator will return true if the two tested operands are not equal.

The "<=>" operator returns a value of -1, 0 or 1 depending wether the left side is less than, equal to or greater than the right side.

"Greater than" operators compare two operands and will return true if the first is greater in value than the second.

"Less than" operators make the same comparison but return true if the first operand is less in value than the second.

Adding the "=" operator after a "greater than" or "less than" operator makes it also return true if the two operands are exactly equal in value.

Numeric Comparison Examples

Edit	Run

```perl
1  #!/usr/bin/perl
2
3  $six = 6; $ten = 10;
4  $is_equal  = ($six == $six);
5  $not_equal = ($six != $ten);
6  $comp1 = ($six <=> $ten);
7  $comp2 = ($six <=> $six);
8  $comp3 = ($ten <=> $six);
9  $greater = ($ten > $six);
10 $less     = ($six < $ten);
11
12 print <<"DOC";
13 content-type: text/html\n\n <html>
14 <li>Is Equal  = $is_equal
15 <li>Not Equal = $not_equal
16 <li>Comparison #1 = $comp1
17 <li>Comparison #2 = $comp2
18 <li>Comparison #3 = $comp3
19 <li>Greater = $greater
20 <li>Less = $less </html>
21 DOC
```

The boolean value of true is represented by the number 1.

As Text	In Browser

- Is Equal = 1
- Not Equal = 1
- Comparison #1 = -1
- Comparison #2 = 0
- Comparison #3 = 1
- Greater = 1
- Less = 1

String Operators

The operators that are commonly used in Perl to compare string values are all listed in the table below together with some useful string manipulation features:

The "Greater Than" and "Less Than" operators convert strings to their ASCII values then compare the totals.

Operator	Operation
eq	Equality
ne	Not equal
gt	Greater Than
lt	Less Than
cmp	Returns -1, 0 or 1 depending on comparison
.	Concatenation
x	Repeat
uc(string)	Convert to Upper Case
lc(string)	Convert to Lower Case
chr(number)	Get the character of an ASCII number
ord(character)	Get the ASCII number of a character

See page 28 for more on the concatenation operator.

The string comparison operators are the equivalent of the numeric operators "==" (eq), "!=" (ne), ">" (gt), "<" (lt) and "<=>" (cmp).

Repeating strings can be performed with the "x" operator although in reality it is seldom found.

Strings may be forced to be lowercase for comparison using the lc() function.

The chr() and ord() functions can be used to manipulate individual characters by their associated ASCII code number where, for example, "A" is 65.

String Operator Examples

```
Edit    Run

 1 #!/usr/bin/perl
 2
 3 $is_equal   = "Perl" eq "Perl";
 4 $compare    = "Perl" cmp "perl";
 5 $repeat     = "Perl " x 5;
 6 $uppercase = uc("Perl");
 7 $lowercase = lc("Perl");
 8 $number     = ord("P");
 9 $character = chr(80);
10
11 print <<"DOC";
12 content-type: text/html\n\n <html>
13 <li>Equality = $is_equal
14 <li>Comparison =$compare
15 <li>Repetition = $repeat
16 <li>Uppercase = $uppercase
17 <li>Lowercase = $lowercase
18 <li>ASCII Number = $number
19 <li>ASCII Character = $character
20 </html>
21 DOC
```

```
As Text   In Browser

   • Equality = 1
   • Comparison =-1
   • Repetition = Perl Perl Perl Perl Perl
   • Uppercase = PERL
   • Lowercase = perl
   • ASCII Number = 80
   • ASCII Character = P
```

Conditional Operator

The Perl coder's favourite comparison operator is probably the conditional operator. This first evaluates an expression for a true or false value then executes one of two given statements depending on the result of the evaluation.

The conditional operator has this syntax:

```
(test expression) ? if true do this : if false do this;
```

The example below tests the $is_true and $is_false variables then executes the appropriate statements:

```
Edit    Run

 1 #!/usr/bin/perl
 2
 3 $is_true = 1;
 4 $is_false = 0;
 5 $result1 = ($is_true)?"Red":"Green";
 6 $result2 = ($is_false)?"Red":"Green";
 7
 8 print <<"DOC";
 9 content-type: text/html\n\n
10 <html> <h4>Conditional Operator</h4>
11 <li>True Colour is $result1
12 <li>False Colour is $result2
13 </html>
14 DOC
```

As Text | In Browser

Conditional Operator
- True Colour is Red
- False Colour is Green

Range Operator

The range operator is useful to return a list of values counting in ones from the left operand to the right operand.

It is also useful to define the number of iterations that a loop should make. This example makes 10 iterations:

See page 51 for more examples of looping scripts.

```
for(1..10){ print "Perl" }
```

The script below stores the range of characters in the alphabet in an array variable then prints it to be displayed:

Array variables are just variables that can hold more than one value – see chapter 5 on arrays.

Edit	Run

```
 1 #!/usr/bin/perl
 2
 3 @lc_alphabet = ("a".."z");
 4 @uc_alphabet = ("A".."Z");
 5 @numbers = (1..10);
 6
 7 print <<"DOC";
 8 content-type: text/html\n\n
 9 <html><h4>Range Operator</h4>
10 <font face="arial narrow">
11 @lc_alphabet <br>
12 @uc_alphabet <br>
13 @numbers </font>
14 </html>
15 DOC
```

As Text	In Browser

Range Operator

abcdefghijklmnopqrstuvwxyz
ABCDEFGHIJKLMNOPQRSTUVWXYZ
1 2 3 4 5 6 7 8 9 10

Math Functions

Perl has a number of intrinsic functions available for performing Mathematical calculations as listed in this table:

Function	Operation
abs()	Return the absolute value
atan2(y,x)	Return the arctangent of y /x
cos()	Return the cosine
hex()	Return decimal value of a hexidecimal string
oct()	Return decimal value of an octal string
sin()	Return the sine
sqrt()	Return the square root

All these functions will perform a mathematical calculation on a value placed inside the brackets after the function name.

Atan2() returns the angle, in radians, from the X axis to a point at the position (y,x) in the range -PI to PI.

The value will be negative if y is negative and positive if y is positive. The result will be zero if y is zero.

The abs(), cos(), sin() and sqrt() functions all act as expected.

The hex() function is used in the form parser code on page 128.

Notice that the hex() and oct() functions are used to convert values from hexadecimal and octal, rather than into those formats.

Web browsers will automatically convert some data into hexadecimal values before sending it to a CGI script.

The hex() function is important to convert that data back into decimal format so it can be more easily handled in the script.

Each of these functions is demonstrated by the examples on the facing page.

Math Function Examples

Edit | Run

```perl
1  #!/usr/bin/perl
2
3  $absolute = abs(-100);
4  $arc = atan2(100,200);
5  $cosine = cos(100);
6  $from_hex = hex(10);
7  $from_oct = oct(10);
8  $sine = sin(100);
9  $sq_root = sqrt(144);
10
11 print <<"DOC";
12 content-type:text/html\n\n
13 <html>
14 <li>Absolute is $absolute
15 <li>Arc is $arc
16 <li>Cosine is $cosine
17 <li>From Hexidecimal is $from_hex
18 <li>From Octal is $from_oct
19 <li>Sine is $sine
20 <li>Square Root is $sq_root
21 </html>
22 DOC
```

As Text | In Browser

- Absolute is 100
- Arc is 0.463647609000806
- Cosine is 0.862318872287684
- From Hexidecimal is 16
- From Octal is 8
- Sine is -0.50365641109759
- Square Root is 12

Escape Sequences

When a character in a string is preceded by the backslash character "\" there is a special effect on the character immediately following the backslash.

This is known as an escape sequence as it allows the character to escape recognition as part of the Perl syntax. The table below lists common escape sequences:

\n	New line
\l	Lower case next character
\u	Upper case next character
\L	Lower case unti \E is found
\U	Upper case until \E is found
\'	Single quote that will not terminate a string
\"	Double quote that will not terminate a string
\\	Single backslash character

Paired single quotes may be nested inside double quotes without the backslash escape character.

The escape sequence " \" " is useful to incorporate quotation marks within a string without the string being terminated.

In the code below several escape sequences are used to format the text and permit the use of nested quotes without terminating the string prematurely:

```perl
$ln1 = "We say \"Perl is Cool\" ";
$ln2 = "\\ \ulet\'s have \Umore.\E";

print "content-type:text/html\n\n<html>$ln1$ln2</html>";
```

| As Text | In Browser |

We say "Perl is Cool" \ Let's have MORE.

Making Statements

This chapter shows by example how to write statements in Perl script. Conditional branching is demonstrated and each type of loop statement is explained and illustrated.

Covers

Chapter Four

Conditional If

A statement is simply any valid Perl code that will perform some action within a script.

The "if" keyword is used to perform the basic conditional Perl test to evaluate an expression for a boolean value.

The statement following the evaluation will only be executed when the expression returns true.

The syntax for the "if" statement looks like this:

```
if(test expression) { statement to be executed if true }
```

Curly brackets are also known as "braces".

Notice that the test expression must be enclosed in standard brackets. The statement must be enclosed in curly brackets.

The example below contains two conditional tests but only the statement following the test returning true is executed:

```
Edit    Run
  1  #!/usr/bin/perl
  2
  3  $sky="blue";
  4
  5  print "content-type:text/html\n\n";
  6  print "<html>The weather is ";
  7
  8  if($sky eq "grey") {print "dull."};
  9  if($sky eq "blue") {print "fine."};
 10
 11  print "</html>";
```

```
As Text   In Browser

The weather is fine.
```

Multiple Statements

The curly brackets that follow a conditional test may contain more than one statement.

When the test returns true all statements that are enclosed within the curly brackets after the test will be executed.

The following example builds on the previous example to add multiple statements to be executed after a true test:

The code inside the curly brackets is the "statement block".

```
Edit    Run
 1 #!/usr/bin/perl
 2
 3 $sky="blue";
 4
 5 if($sky eq "blue"){
 6 $weather="sunny"; $mood="happy";
 7 }
 8
 9 if($sky eq "grey"){
10 $weather="overcast";
11 $mood="subdued";
12 }
13
14 print <<"DOC";
15 content-type:text/html\n\n  <html>
16 Today the weather is $weather <br>
17 and everyone is $mood.     </html>
18 DOC
```

As Text   In Browser

Today the weather is sunny and everyone is happy.

Else Alternative

The Perl keyword "else" is used with an "if" conditional test to provide alternative code that will be executed when the test returns false.

This arrangement determines the direction that the script takes when run and is known as "conditional branching".

In the following example the script tests two numbers to determine if they are odd or even then writes the appropriate result in the html code:

Notice that the terminating semi-colon can be omitted after the final statement in curly brackets.

```
Edit  |  Run  |

 1 #!/usr/bin/perl
 2
 3 $num1=10;
 4 $num2=11;
 5
 6 print "content-type:text/html\n\n";
 7 print "<html>";
 8
 9 if($num1 % 2 == 0)
10      {print "\$num1 is even. <br>"}
11 else {print "\$num1 is odd. <br>"}
12
13 if($num2 % 2 == 0)
14      {print "\$num2 is even."}
15 else {print "\$num2 is odd."}
16
17 print "</html>";
```

Remember to escape the "$" character with a backslash to use it literally.

```
As Text | In Browser |

$num1 is even.
$num2 is odd.
```

Elsif Alternative

An "if" block may test multiple alternatives with the "elsif" Perl keyword. This combines an "else" alternative with a new "if" conditional test.

The script will test each condition until a test returns true.

Statements associated with that test will then be executed and no more code is parsed in that "if" block.

This is demonstrated in the example below which returns true at the first "elsif" conditional test. Its associated $shade variable is assigned the string value of "navy" then parsing ends in this "if" block.

The final "else" statement in this block is used to set default values in the event that none of the preceding tests return true.

```perl
1  #!/usr/bin/perl
2
3  $hue="blue";
4
5  if($hue eq "red"){$shade="crimson"}
6  elsif($hue eq "blue"){$shade="navy"}
7  elsif($hue eq "blue"){$shade="royal"}
8  else {$hue="yellow"; $shade="lemon"}
9
10 print <<"DOC";
11 content-type:text/html\n\n
12 <html>
13 Shade is $shade
14 </html>
15 DOC
```

Edit | Run

The spelling of "elsif" has only a single "e" and is not "elseif".

As Text | In Browser

Shade is navy

For Loop

The "for" loop is probably the most frequently used type of loop that is found in Perl scripts and has this syntax:

```
for(initializer, test, increment/decrement) {statements}
```

The code contained in the statement block will be executed at each "pass" or "iteration" of the loop.

The initializer is used to set the starting value of a counter that keeps track of the number of loop iterations.

A variable is declared to act as the counter and is assigned a value that is the starting point of the loop.

Traditionally the variable used as the counter is named "$i".

To start a loop counting from zero the initializer would be declared with $i=0.

At each iteration of the loop a conditional test is made and the loop will only continue if the test returns true.

If the test returns false then the loop will end.

The conditional test commonly specifies an end point for the loop by setting an extreme limit for the counter value.

When counting up, the "less than" operator "<" will return true until the counter's upper limit is reached.

When counting down the "greater than" operator ">" will return true until the counter's lower limit is reached.

Because the loop starts at zero, not one, the limit is the same number as the number of iterations.

To loop ten times in an incrementing loop starting at zero the conditional test would be declared with $i<10.

With every iteration of a "for" loop the value of the counter variable is incremented, or decremented. If the conditional test still returns true the statement block is then executed.

The example on the facing page makes ten iterations and changes the assigned value of two variables at each pass.

For Loop Example

Placing the increment or decrement operators before an operand immediately returns its new value. Change ++$up to $up++ to see the difference.

```
Edit | Run |

 1 #!/usr/bin/perl
 2
 3 $up=0;
 4 $dn=0;
 5
 6 print "content-type:text/html\n\n";
 7 print "<html>";
 8
 9 for($i=0; $i<10; $i++){
10 ++$up;
11 --$dn;
12 print "<li>Rising is $up ";
13 print "Falling is $dn";
14 }
15
16 print "</html>";
```

As Text | In Browser |

- Rising is 1 Falling is -1
- Rising is 2 Falling is -2
- Rising is 3 Falling is -3
- Rising is 4 Falling is -4
- Rising is 5 Falling is -5
- Rising is 6 Falling is -6
- Rising is 7 Falling is -7
- Rising is 8 Falling is -8
- Rising is 9 Falling is -9
- Rising is 10 Falling is -10

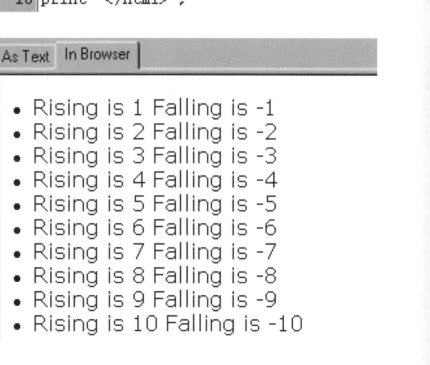

Conditional Unless

Another conditional test can be made using the "unless" Perl keyword to preclude the execution of a statement when the test returns true.

An "if" conditional test could be used for this purpose but the code is simpler and more elegant using "unless" instead.

The example below would normally print a list from 1 to 9 but the "unless" statement precludes all the even numbers:

In this example the equivalent conditional test can be made using this code:

if ((\$i % 2 == 0) ==0)

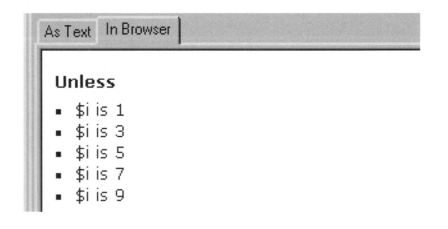

```perl
Edit    Run

1  #!/usr/bin/perl
2
3  print "content-type:text/html\n\n";
4  print "<html><h4>Unless</h4>";
5
6  for($i=1; $i<10; $i++)
7  {
8    unless($i % 2 == 0)
9    {
10     print "<li>\$i is $i";
11   }
12 }
13 print "</html>";
```

As Text | In Browser

Unless

- \$i is 1
- \$i is 3
- \$i is 5
- \$i is 7
- \$i is 9

Until Loop

The Perl "until" keyword can be used to make a simple loop.

An "until" loop performs a conditional test then, if the test returns false, will execute the code in its statement block.

This continues until the test returns true and the loop ends.

In this example the print statement is executed and the variable is incremented on each iteration. When the variable value reaches 6 the test returns true and the loop ends.

There must always be an expression in the statement block that changes the tested value. Otherwise the loop becomes an "infinite loop" that will never end.

```perl
Edit | Run

 1 #!/usr/bin/perl
 2
 3 print "content-type:text/html\n\n";
 4 print "<html><h4>Until Loop</h4>";
 5
 6 $count=1;
 7
 8 until($count==6)
 9 {
10   print "<li>Count is $count";
11   $count++;
12 }
13 print "</html>";
```

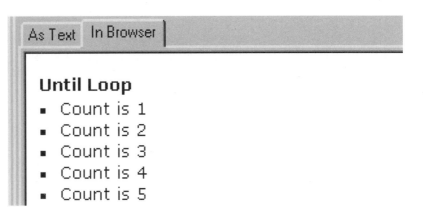

As Text | In Browser

Until Loop
- Count is 1
- Count is 2
- Count is 3
- Count is 4
- Count is 5

While Loop

The Perl "while" keyword can be used to make a loop similar to an "until" loop but with one major difference.

With "until" the loop continues until the test returns true whereas a "while" loop continues until the test returns false.

A "while" loop performs a conditional test then, if the test returns true, will execute the code in its statement block.

In this example the print statement is executed and the variable is incremented on each iteration. When the variable value reaches 6 the test returns false and the loop ends.

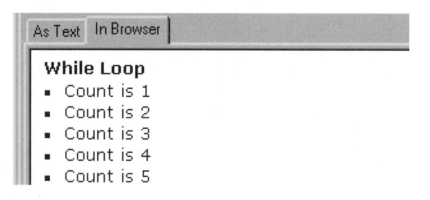

```
Edit    Run

 1  #!/usr/bin/perl
 2
 3  print "content-type:text/html\n\n";
 4  print "<html><h4>While Loop</h4>";
 5
 6  $count=1;
 7  while($count < 6)
 8  {
 9     print "<li>Count is $count";
10     $count++;
11  }
12  print "</html>";
```

As Text | In Browser

While Loop
- Count is 1
- Count is 2
- Count is 3
- Count is 4
- Count is 5

Do Loop

A "do" loop is unusual in having its conditional test after the statement block. This means that the statements contained in a "do" loop will always run at least once.

The "do" loop can use either a "while" statement or an "until" statement as its conditional test.

In the example below a "while" statement tests the $count variable value and ends the loop when this value reaches 6.

Because "while" statements are commonly used to test in "do" loops this loop is also known as "do-while".

```
Edit    Run

 1  #!/usr/bin/perl
 2
 3  print "content-type:text/html\n\n";
 4  print "<html><h4>Do Loop</h4>";
 5
 6  $count=1;
 7  do{
 8      print "<li>Count is $count";
 9      $count++;
10  }
11  while($count<6);
12
13  print "</html>";
```

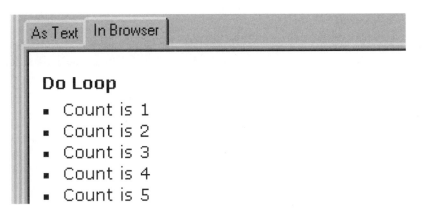

As Text   In Browser

Do Loop

- Count is 1
- Count is 2
- Count is 3
- Count is 4
- Count is 5

Next Jump

The Perl "next" keyword is used to stop the current iteration of any loop and then continue with the loop's next iteration.

It is useful to prevent the execution of statements for an iteration when a certain test condition is met.

For example, the script below illustrates a "for" loop that would normally write a Html line at every pass.

The "next" statement prevents the execution of the print statement for the iteration when the tested value is 3.

However, the loop does continue with the next iteration.

The "next", "last" & "redo" statements all jump to a previous point in the script so are known as "jump statements".

```
Edit    Run

 1  #!/usr/bin/perl
 2
 3  print "content-type:text/html\n\n";
 4  print "<html><h4>Next Jump</h4>";
 5
 6  for($i=1; $i<6; $i++)
 7  {
 8     if($i==3){ next }
 9     print "<li>Count is is $i";
10  }
11  print "</html>";
```

```
As Text   In Browser

Next Jump
  ▪ Count is is 1
  ▪ Count is is 2
  ▪ Count is is 4
  ▪ Count is is 5
```

Last Jump

The "last" Perl keyword is used to stop the current iteration of any loop and exit the loop without any further passes.

This is useful to terminate a loop instantly when a certain test condition has been met.

For example, the script below illustrates a "while" loop that would normally write a Html line at every pass.

The "last" statement prevents the execution of the print statement for the iteration when the tested value is 4.

The loop ends and does not continue with the next iteration.

The "last" statement must come before other statements in the statement block to avoid them being executed.

```
Edit    Run

 1  #!/usr/bin/perl
 2
 3  print "content-type:text/html\n\n";
 4  print "<html><h4>Last Jump</h4>";
 5
 6  $count=1;
 7  while($count < 6)
 8  {
 9      if($count==4) { last }
10      print "<li>Count is $count";
11      $count++;
12  }
13  print "</html>";
```

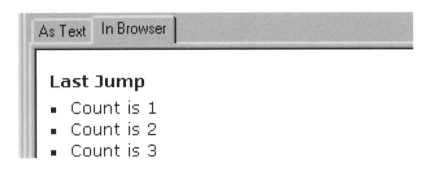

As Text   In Browser

Last Jump

- Count is 1
- Count is 2
- Count is 3

Redo Jump

The "redo" Perl keyword can be placed at the end of a statement block to repeat its execution.

This creates a loop by iterating the statements code repeatedly. It is important to create a means of exit in order to avoid creating an infinite loop.

The example below uses a "last" statement as a way to exit.

A loop of this kind is seldom found in reality. It is included here to illustrate the adage that "Perl always has more than one way to do anything".

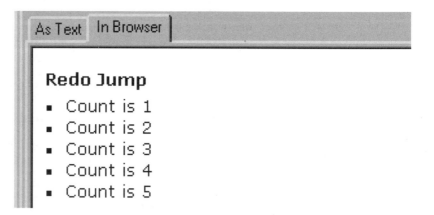

```perl
#!/usr/bin/perl

print "content-type:text/html\n\n";
print "<html><h4>Redo Jump</h4>";

$count=1;
{
   if($count>5) { last }
   print "<li>Count is $count";
   $count++;
   redo;
}
print "</html>";
```

As Text | In Browser

Redo Jump

- Count is 1
- Count is 2
- Count is 3
- Count is 4
- Count is 5

Using Arrays

This chapter is devoted to the array variable. Unlike the scalar variable that holds a single value an array can contain multiple pieces of data. The examples given here show how to manipulate the data contained in array variables.

Covers

Chapter Five

Create An Array

An array is declared in Perl with the "@" character followed by a given name. The designated name should use the same naming conventions that apply when naming scalar variables.

Naming rules for variables are discussed on page 22.

A list of data items can then be assigned to the array variable using the "=" character followed by the list within brackets.

The items in the list must be separated by commas and string items must be enclosed within quotes.

Because the assignation of single word lists is common, Perl has a special inbuilt function "qw()" that permits the words to be listed without quotes and separated only by a space.

This example declares three arrays and assigns lists to them:

The "@" symbol is a reminder of the "A" in "Array".

```
Edit    Run

 1 #!/usr/bin/perl
 2
 3 @words1=("dog","cat","bird","fish");
 4 @words2=qw(dog cat bird fish);
 5 @numbrs=(1,2,3,4.567);
 6
 7 print <<"DOC";
 8 content-type:text/html\n\n
 9 <html>
10 <li>@words1 <li>@words2 <li>@numbrs
11 </html>
12 DOC
```

As Text | In Browser

- dog cat bird fish
- dog cat bird fish
- 1 2 3 4.567

Referencing Elements

The list of items stored in an array are referred to as "elements" and are numerically indexed starting at zero.

Each element can be referenced using its index number contained within square brackets after the array name.

The array name must be preceded by the "$" character when addressing single pieces of data, not the "@" array symbol.

Assigning an array to a scalar assigns the total array length.

Elements can also be addressed backwards from the last element starting at -1 as illustrated in this example:

The first element in an array is index number zero, not index one.

```
    Edit    Run

     1  #!/usr/bin/perl
     2
     3  @words=("dog","cat","bird","fish");
     4  $wordslength=@words;
     5
     6  print <<"DOC";
     7  content-type:text/html\n\n
     8  <html>
     9  <li>First element is $words[0]
    10  <li>Final element is $words[-1]
    11  at index number $#words
    12  <li>Array length is $wordslength
    13  </html>
    14  DOC
```

```
   As Text   In Browser


     ▪ First element is dog
     ▪ Final element is fish at index number 3
     ▪ Array length is 4
```

Convert Scalar To Array

The intrinsic Perl function "split()" can be used to fill the elements of an array from a $scalar value.

This function requires two arguments to specify the scalar name and at what points the scalar value should be split.

If the scalar value is a text string with single spaces between the words then the string can be split by specifying the space as the points at which to split the scalar.

If the value is a list separated by commas then the comma can be specified as the point at which to split.

Specify the point between two forward-slash characters when defining the argument as seen in this example:

Notice that the output will automatically supply a space between the element values.

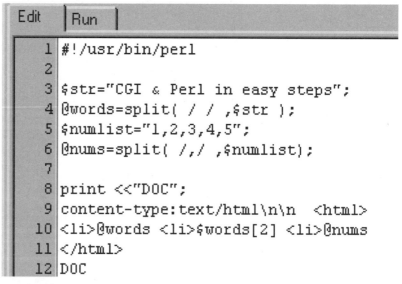

```
1  #!/usr/bin/perl
2
3  $str="CGI & Perl in easy steps";
4  @words=split( / / ,$str );
5  $numlist="1,2,3,4,5";
6  @nums=split( /,/ ,$numlist);
7
8  print <<"DOC";
9  content-type:text/html\n\n  <html>
10 <li>@words <li>$words[2] <li>@nums
11 </html>
12 DOC
```

As Text | In Browser

- CGI & Perl in easy steps
- Perl
- 1 2 3 4 5

Fill Elements Loop

A loop can be used to efficiently fill the elements of an array by assigning a value to each element in turn.

The first loop iteration can address the first array element and assign a value to it. On the next iteration the second element can be assigned a value. This process continues until all the data has been stored inside array elements.

In the example below a "for" loop runs 5 iterations.

Each iteration assigns a concatenated string value to successive elements then writes them into an Html list.

The array will expand in size to have the number of elements that is required for the data.

```
Edit    Run

 1  #!/usr/bin/perl
 2
 3  print "content-type:text/html\n\n";
 4  print "<html>";
 5
 6  for($i=0; $i<5; $i++)
 7  {
 8      $arr[$i]="Element Number ".$i;
 9      print "<li>$arr[$i]";
10  }
11
12  print "</html>";
```

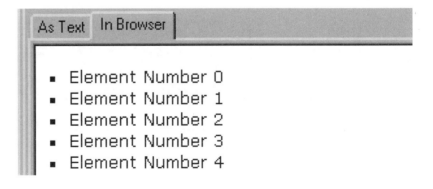

As Text | In Browser

- Element Number 0
- Element Number 1
- Element Number 2
- Element Number 3
- Element Number 4

Address All Elements

The "foreach" Perl keyword is used to create a special kind of loop that will list each element value in an array variable.

Each element value is assigned to a single scalar variable in succession on each iteration of the loop.

The current value contained by the scalar variable can be used within the loop's statement block to process that element's data.

In the example below each element value is assigned to a variable named $pet then written into a Html list:

The way that the curly brackets are positioned in this example is the recognised normal format. Examples given in this book may use other formats in order to clarify the code.

```perl
Edit    Run

  1 #!/usr/bin/perl
  2
  3 @pets=("dog","cat","bird","fish");
  4
  5 print "content-type:text/html\n\n";
  6 print "<html><h4>Foreach Loop</h4>";
  7
  8 foreach $pet (@pets){
  9 print "<li> $pet";
 10 }
 11
 12 print "</html>";
```

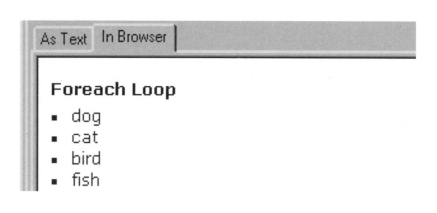

As Text | In Browser

Foreach Loop

- dog
- cat
- bird
- fish

Subarrays

A subarray is an array whose element values have been assigned from selected elements of another array.

Multiple selected elements of an array can be addressed using the square brackets that follow the array name.

The "$" character is only used to address single items of data.

The index numbers must be separated by a comma. Also the array name should be preceded by the "@" symbol because it addresses multiple items of data.

The example below creates an array of weekday names then assigns selected ones to a subarray.

The Html output displays the weekday names array, the subarray and a further multiple selection:

Addressing from the end of the array, the subarray could be assigned the same selected elements with @subarray=@arr[-5,-3,-1];

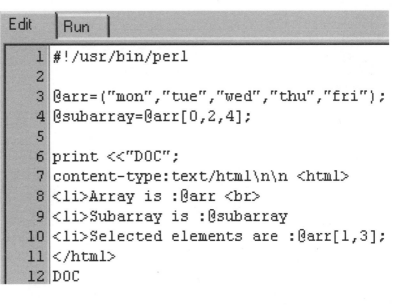

```perl
#!/usr/bin/perl

@arr=("mon","tue","wed","thu","fri");
@subarray=@arr[0,2,4];

print <<"DOC";
content-type:text/html\n\n <html>
<li>Array is :@arr <br>
<li>Subarray is :@subarray
<li>Selected elements are :@arr[1,3];
</html>
DOC
```

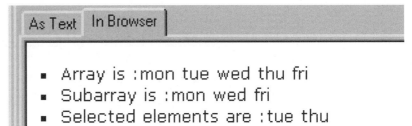

As Text | In Browser

- Array is :mon tue wed thu fri
- Subarray is :mon wed fri
- Selected elements are :tue thu

Add/Remove First Element

The Perl "unshift()" function is used to add new elements at the beginning of an existing array.

It takes two arguments to specify the name of the array and the value that will become the new element. The value to be added can be defined as a string, a number or a scalar.

Multiple new leading elements can also be added by specifying the value to be added as another array.

The Perl "shift()" function just takes the array name as its argument and will remove the first element of that array.

In this example an array of three elements is first created. Then the "unshift()" function adds a new first element. Finally the "shift()" function removes the new first element:

The "shift()" function returns the removed element value. This can be assigned to a scalar in the same way as the "pop()" function in the example on the facing page.

```
    Edit    Run
    1  #!/usr/bin/perl
    2
    3  print "content-type:text/html\n\n";
    4  print "<html>";
    5  @arr=("tue","wed","thu");
    6  print "<li>Original array is : @arr";
    7  unshift(@arr,"mon");
    8  print "<li>Array is now : @arr";
    9  shift(@arr);
   10  print "<li>Array is back to : @arr";
   11  print "</html>";
```

```
    As Text   In Browser

      • Original array is : tue wed thu
      • Array is now : mon tue wed thu
      • Array is back to : tue wed thu
```

Add/Remove Last Element

The Perl "push()" functions adds to the end of an existing array and the "pop()" function removes the final element.

They work just like "unshift()" and "shift()" functions do except they perform at the end of an array.

In the example below "push()" adds the elements of a second array onto the end of those already in the original array. Then "pop()" removes the last element and stores its value:

This example uses the Range operator to fill both sets of array elements.
See page 43 for details.

```perl
Edit    Run

 1 #!/usr/bin/perl
 2
 3 print "content-type:text/html\n\n";
 4 print "<html>";
 5
 6 @count=(1..5); @extra=(6..10);
 7 print "<li>First Half : @count";
 8
 9 push(@count, @extra);
10 print "<li>Full Count : @count";
11
12 $store=pop(@count);
13 print "<li>One Removed : @count";
14 print "<li>Removed Value : $store";
15
16 print "</html>";
```

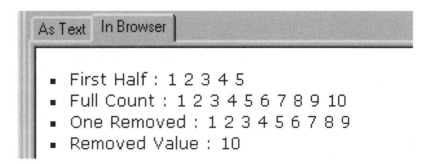

```
As Text   In Browser

  ▪ First Half : 1 2 3 4 5
  ▪ Full Count : 1 2 3 4 5 6 7 8 9 10
  ▪ One Removed : 1 2 3 4 5 6 7 8 9
  ▪ Removed Value : 10
```

Combining Arrays

Multiple arrays can be assigned to a new array to create an array with their combined element values.

The arrays to be assigned must be contained within brackets and separated by a comma.

In this example the script first creates two arrays with three elements in each array. These are then assigned to a new array to create an array with their combined element values.

The combined element values are shown in a Html table:

More than two arrays can be combined with this process. For example, 3 arrays can be combined with @com=(@arr1,@arr2,@arr3)

```perl
Edit    Run

 1 #!/usr/bin/perl
 2
 3 @arr1=("cat","dog","bird");
 4 @arr2=("man","woman","child");
 5 @combined=(@arr1,@arr2);
 6
 7 print <<"DOC";
 8 content-type:text/html\n\n
 9 <html>
10 <table border=2 cellpadding=2>
11 <tr><td align=center>
12 <b>Combined Arrays:</b><br>
13 @combined </td></tr></table>
14 </html>
15 DOC
```

As Text   In Browser

> **Combined Arrays:**
> cat dog bird man woman child

Replacing Elements

Individual element values can be replaced by addressing the element and simply assigning a new value to it.

Multiple element values can be replaced using their array index numbers separated by a comma.

The assignations must be within brackets and also separated by a comma.

In the following example an array first has a single element value replaced, then multiple element values are replaced:

```
Edit | Run

 1 #!/usr/bin/perl
 2
 3 @arr=("cat","dog","bird");
 4 print "content-type:text/html\n\n";
 5 print "<html>";
 6
 7 print "<li>Original array is : @arr";
 8 $arr[0]="fish";
 9
10 print "<li>Amended array is : @arr";
11 @arr[1,2]=("and","chips");
12
13 print "<li>Final array is : @arr";
14
15 print "</html>";
```

The elements need not be consecutive so any index numbers can be specified and in any order.

```
As Text | In Browser

 • Original array is : cat dog bird
 • Amended array is : fish dog bird
 • Final array is : fish and chips
```

Sort Alphabetically

The Perl "sort" function can be used to alphabetically arrange the element values of an array.

This function is followed by curly brackets that contain a comparison routine to sort the element values.

For comparison the element values are temporarily passed to scalars named $a and $b then the "cmp" operator performs the alphabetical comparison.

The "sort" function does not directly change the original array elements but the sorted element values can be assigned to a new array.

This example illustrates both forward and backward sorting:

For more details on the "cmp" operator see page 38.

Edit	Run

```
 1  #!/usr/bin/perl
 2
 3  @pets=("cat","dog","bird","animals");
 4  @petsfwd=sort{$a cmp $b}@pets;
 5  @petsback=sort{$b cmp $a}@pets;
 6
 7  print "Content-type: text/html\n\n";
 8  print "<html>";
 9  print "<li>The pets are: @pets";
10  print "<li>Alphabetically: @petsfwd";
11  print "<li>Reverse Order: @petsback";
12  print "</html>";
```

As Text	In Browser

- The pets are: cat dog bird animals
- Alphabetically: animals bird cat dog
- Reverse Order: dog cat bird animals

Sort Numerically

Perl's "sort" function can also be used to arrange the numerical element values of an array.

The operation works in precisely the same manner as the alphabetical sorting example on the facing page.

Again the element values are temporarily passed to scalars named $a and $b for comparison but now the "<=>" operator performs the numerical comparison.

The sorted element values can be assigned to a new array but the "sort" function does not directly change the original array elements.

Here the example shows ascending and descending sorting:

For more details on the "<=>" operator see page 38.

```
Edit    Run

 1  #!/usr/bin/perl
 2
 3  @nums=(3,1,6,2,10,7,4,9,5,8);
 4  @nums1=sort{$a <=> $b}@nums;
 5  @nums2=sort{$b <=> $a}@nums;
 6
 7  print "Content-type: text/html\n\n";
 8  print "<html>";
 9  print "<li>The numbers are: @nums";
10  print "<li>Ascending Order: @nums1";
11  print "<li>Descending Order: @nums2";
12  print "</html>";
```

```
As Text   In Browser

   • The numbers are:  3 1 6 2 10 7 4 9 5 8
   • Ascending Order:  1 2 3 4 5 6 7 8 9 10
   • Descending Order:  10 9 8 7 6 5 4 3 2 1
```

Slice And Reverse

Using multiple selected elements from an array is referred to as taking a "slice" of the array.

The syntax to take a "slice" has the index numbers of the selected elements, separated by commas, inside the square brackets that follow the array name.

In the example script on this page the code takes a slice from the "@arr" array and assigns it to the new array "@slice".

To show how the order of array elements can be reversed the example then demonstrates the Perl "reverse()" function.

The reversed slice is assigned to a new array "@rev" and all three arrays are displayed by the Html code:

The "qw()" function means that the element values do not need any surrounding quotes.

```perl
Edit    Run

 1 #!/usr/bin/perl
 2
 3 @arr=qw(Andrew James David William);
 4 @slice=@arr[0,3];
 5 @rev=reverse(@slice);
 6
 7 print "Content-type: text/html\n\n";
 8 print "<html>";
 9 print "<li>Names : @arr";
10 print "<li>Slice is : @slice";
11 print "<li>Reverse is : @rev";
12 print "</html>";
```

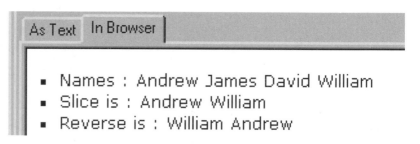

As Text   In Browser

- Names : Andrew James David William
- Slice is : Andrew William
- Reverse is : William Andrew

Using Hashes

This chapter is devoted to the hash variable type that is so important to handling Html form data in CGI scripts. A hash variable is a special type of array that arranges its data in pairs that form an "associative array". The examples in this chapter demonstrate how to usefully handle the hash data pairs in Perl scripts.

Covers

Chapter Six

Key-Value Pairs

Hash variables are a special type of array that stores data in associated pairs, known as an "associative array".

This is a particularly useful variable for handling Html form data when it is sent from the web page to a CGI script on the server. The form data is sent as pairs in which the key is the form field name and the value is the data in that field.

The "o"s in the "%" symbol are a reminder of the pairs inside hash arrays.

A hash array is declared using the "%" symbol followed by a given name with the usual variable naming conventions.

Perl can access the associated value of a hash pair by specifying its key name.

The syntax to access a single hash value requires that the "$" character is used in front of the hash name. The required key name is specified in the curly brackets that follow the hash name.

This example creates a hash containing two pairs then the Html displays the values associated with the key names:

```
Edit | Run
1 #!/usr/bin/perl
2
3 %hsh=("bird","Swan","fish","Trout");
4 print "content-type: text/html\n\n";
5 print "<html>";
6 print "<li>Bird is $hsh{bird}";
7 print "<li>Fish is $hsh{fish}";
8 print "</html>";
```

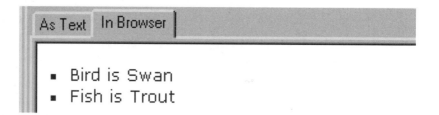

```
As Text | In Browser

  ▪ Bird is Swan
  ▪ Fish is Trout
```

Hash Slices

A slice of selected hash variables can be assigned in a similar way to that of a regular array.

The only difference is that the value's key is used to address each required element instead of using an index number.

When referencing a hash slice the "@" symbol must precede the hash key name in order to address multiple values.

The hash key name is followed by curly brackets containing the required hash key names. All the key names must be enclosed in quotes and separated by a comma.

The example below defines a hash array then assigns two slices from it to new array variables:

Hash key names that are integers do not need to be enclosed in quotes when addressing their associated values.

```perl
   Edit    Run

    1  #!/usr/bin/perl
    2
    3  %hsh=qw( r red g green b blue );
    4
    5  @slice1=@hsh{"r","b"};
    6  @slice2=@hsh{"g","r"};
    7
    8  print "Content-type: text/html\n\n";
    9  print "<html>";
   10  print "<li>Slice 1 is @slice1 ";
   11  print "<li>Slice 2 is @slice2 ";
   12  print "</html>";
```

```
   As Text    In Browser


    ■  Slice 1 is red blue
    ■  Slice 2 is green red
```

Get All Keys

The Perl "keys()" function is useful to get all the key names from inside a hash array.

A single argument is required with this function to specify the name of the hash to get the key names from.

This example first creates two hash arrays whose elements are then concatenated into a new third array called "%both".

The key name of each pair is displayed by the Html code.

| Edit | Run |

```perl
1  #!/usr/bin/perl
2
3  %hsh1= qw( R Red G Green B Blue );
4  %hsh2= qw( Y Yellow P Purple );
5  %both= ( %hsh1, %hsh2 );
6
7  @arr1=keys(%hsh1);
8  @arr2=keys(%hsh2);
9  @allkeys=keys(%both);
10
11 print "Content-type: text/html\n\n";
12 print "<html>";
13 print "<li>Hash 1 keys are: @arr1";
14 print "<li>Hash 2 keys are: @arr2";
15 print "<li>All keys are: @allkeys";
16 print "</html>";
```

The order of the elements is not maintained as the "@arr1" array does not store the key names in the given order of R,G,B.

| As Text | In Browser |

- Hash 1 keys are: G B R
- Hash 2 keys are: P Y
- All keys are: G P Y R B

Get All Values

The Perl "values()" function is a similar function to the "keys()" function.

All the values in a hash array can be retrieved using the "values()" function.

The hash name that contains the required values is specified as the single argument to the "values()" function.

The example displays the values of each pair:

Although the pairs may not be in their original order the keys are still associated with their proper values.

```
Edit    Run

 1  #!/usr/bin/perl
 2
 3  %hsh1= qw( R Red G Green B Blue );
 4  %hsh2= qw( Y Yellow P Purple );
 5  %both= ( %hsh1, %hsh2 );
 6
 7  @arr1=values(%hsh1);
 8  @arr2=values(%hsh2);
 9  @allvals=values(%both);
10
11  print "Content-type: text/html\n\n";
12  print "<html>";
13  print "<li>Hash 1 values are: @arr1";
14  print "<li>Hash 2 values are: @arr2";
15  print "<li>All values are: @allvals";
16  print "</html>";
```

As Text | In Browser

- Hash 1 values are: Green Blue Red
- Hash 2 values are: Purple Yellow
- All values are: Green Purple Yellow Red Blue

Get All Keys And Values

The previous two examples that get keys and values from a hash array can be combined in a loop.

A "foreach" loop gets each successive key and its associated value on each iteration.

The example uses the code from the earlier examples to loop through each key then display the key name and its value:

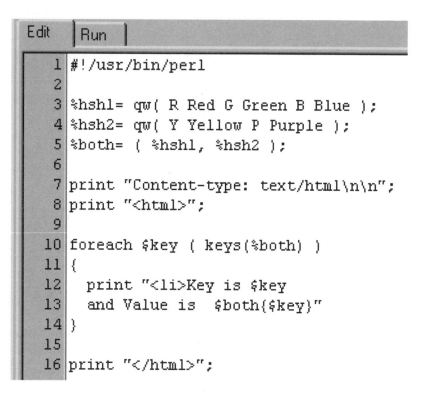

```perl
1  #!/usr/bin/perl
2
3  %hsh1= qw( R Red G Green B Blue );
4  %hsh2= qw( Y Yellow P Purple );
5  %both= ( %hsh1, %hsh2 );
6
7  print "Content-type: text/html\n\n";
8  print "<html>";
9
10 foreach $key ( keys(%both) )
11 {
12    print "<li>Key is $key
13    and Value is  $both{$key}"
14 }
15
16 print "</html>";
```

A "foreach" loop is like a "for" loop that repeats as long as there is another key on the array.

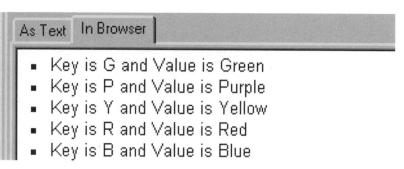

As Text | In Browser

- Key is G and Value is Green
- Key is P and Value is Purple
- Key is Y and Value is Yellow
- Key is R and Value is Red
- Key is B and Value is Blue

Deleting Pairs

The Perl "delete" keyword can be used to remove pairs from within a hash array.

Address the pair to be deleted with the key name enclosed in curly brackets after the hash name.

The hash name should be preceded by a "$" character to denote that a single element is being addressed.

In this example the script deletes two of the pairs from the hash array using the example on the previous page:

The value of a deleted pair can be assigned to a scalar variable if required with $saved= delete{"keyname"}.

```
Edit | Run

 1 #!/usr/bin/perl
 2
 3 %hsh1= qw( R Red G Green B Blue );
 4 %hsh2= qw( Y Yellow P Purple );
 5 %both= ( %hsh1, %hsh2 );
 6
 7 delete $both{"Y"};
 8 delete $both{"G"};
 9
10 print "Content-type: text/html\n\n";
11 print "<html>";
12 foreach $key(keys(%both)){
13   print "<li>Key is $key
14   and Value is  $both{$key}"
15 }
16 print "</html>";
```

```
As Text | In Browser

 • Key is P and Value is Purple
 • Key is R and Value is Red
 • Key is B and Value is Blue
```

Does Key Exist

It is often useful to check a hash array to determine if a particular key exists in order to branch the script.

The Perl "exists" keyword will search a hash array for a key name and return a value of 1 if the key is found.

If the key is not found the "exists" keyword returns 0 – although this may not be apparent unless tested for.

This example specifies the value of a string depending on the result of the search to illustrate this point:

Use an "exists" test with an "if" statement to perform an action if the key is located in the hash.

```perl
Edit    Run

 1 #!/usr/bin/perl
 2
 3 %hsh1= qw( R Red G Green B Blue );
 4 %hsh2= qw( Y Yellow P Purple );
 5 %both= ( %hsh1, %hsh2 );
 6
 7 $check_p=exists $both{"P"};
 8 $check_t=exists $both{"T"};
 9 $num=($check_t==0)?"zero":"one";
10
11 print "Content-type: text/html\n\n";
12 print "<html>";
13 print "<li>Does P exist ? $check_p";
14 print "<li>Does T exist ? $check_t";
15 print "<li>Check \"T\" is $num";
16 print "</html>";
```

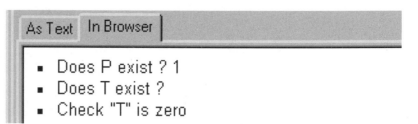

As Text In Browser

- Does P exist ? 1
- Does T exist ?
- Check "T" is zero

Subroutines

This chapter describes by example how subroutines can be useful to define pieces of code that can be repeatedly used in a Perl script.

Covers

Chapter Seven

Define Sub

A "subroutine" is the name for a Perl function that can be called repeatedly from within the main script to execute a statement, or statements, many times.

It is customary to define the subroutines at the end of the main body of the script.

A subroutine is defined with the Perl keyword "sub" followed by a given name for the subroutine. This name should follow the naming conventions used for variables.

The statements to be executed are contained in curly brackets after the subroutine name.

This example defines a subroutine at the end of the script but it is never called in the main body of the script:

```
Edit    Run

 1  #!/usr/bin/perl
 2
 3  print "Content-type: text/html\n\n";
 4  print "<html><b>Subroutines</b><br>";
 5
 6  print "<li>A line from the script";
 7
 8  print "</html>\n";
 9
10  sub greet{
11  print "<li>Hi from the subroutine!";
12  }
```

```
As Text   In Browser

Subroutines
 ▪ A line from the script
```

Call Sub

A subroutine can be called to execute its statements from any point within the main body of the Perl script.

To make the call an ampersand character is used in front of the subroutine name.

It is considered good style to use subroutines widely where a particular action is repeated in the script. Subroutines may perform quite complex actions and can be regarded almost as a "script within a script".

The example below builds on the example on the previous page by adding two calls to the defined subroutine:

```
Edit     Run
 1 #!/usr/bin/perl
 2
 3 print "Content-type: text/html\n\n";
 4 print "<html><b>Subroutines</b><br>";
 5 &greet;
 6 print "<li>A line from the script";
 7 &greet;
 8 print "</html>\n";
 9
10 sub greet{
11 print "<li>Hi from the subroutine!";
12 }
```

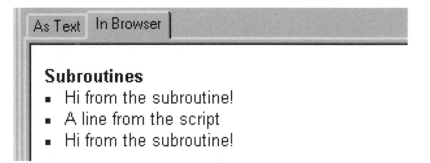

As Text   In Browser

Subroutines
- Hi from the subroutine!
- A line from the script
- Hi from the subroutine!

Passing Value

Like other functions a Perl subroutine can be passed value as an argument from the caller.

The argument as usual is contained in regular brackets that follow the subroutine name in the function call.

Perl automatically stores the arguments passed in a special array called the "underscore array" addressed as "@_".

The first argument value is placed in the underscore array's first element and can be referenced with the syntax "@_[0]".

In the following example a subroutine is defined that will display the value of the single argument passed by the caller:

When only a single argument is passed to the underscore array it can also be addressed as "@_" as well as "$@_[0]".

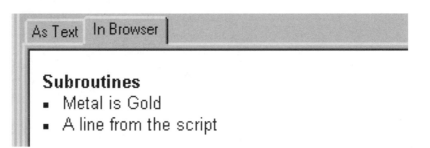

```
Edit    Run

 1 #!/usr/bin/perl
 2
 3 print "Content-type: text/html\n\n";
 4 print "<html><b>Subroutines</b><br>";
 5 &showvalue("Gold");;
 6 print "<li>A line from the script";
 7
 8 print "</html>\n";
 9
10 sub showvalue{
11 print "<li>Metal is $_[0]";
12 }
```

```
As Text   In Browser

Subroutines
  ▪ Metal is Gold
  ▪ A line from the script
```

Multiple Arguments

The caller to a subroutine can pass multiple values to the subroutine as arguments separated by a comma.

These argument values are stored in the special underscore array in sequential elements. So the first value is stored at "@_[0]", the second value at "@_[1]", and so on.

The example below builds on the single value example on the previous page to now pass two values.

In this example a subroutine is defined that will display both values of the two arguments passed by the caller:

```
Edit   Run

 1  #!/usr/bin/perl
 2
 3  print "Content-type: text/html\n\n";
 4  print "<html><b>Subroutines</b><br>";
 5  &showvalue("Gold","Silver");
 6  print "<li>A line from the script";
 7  print "</html>\n";
 8
 9  sub showvalue{
10  print "<li>Metal is $_[0]";
11  print "<li>Metal is $_[1]";
12  }
```

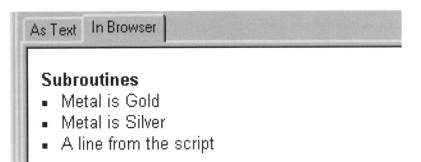

As Text | In Browser

Subroutines
- Metal is Gold
- Metal is Silver
- A line from the script

Library Files

The subroutines in a Perl script may be placed in a separate file called a library. Library files are text files that contain the subroutines and normally have the ".lib" file extension.

The library file does not need a shebang line but must always end with a final "1" to return true to the parser.

This example library is saved with the filename "subs.lib":

The final "1" confirms that the file was successfully accessed.

The library file must be located where Perl can find it.
Examples with the Perl Editor can be placed in the C:\Perl\lib folder.
Examples with Xitami can be placed in C:\Xitami\cgi-bin.

Edit	Run	

```
 1 sub mimetype{
 2 print "Content-type: text/html\n\n";
 3 }
 4
 5 sub dochead{
 6 print "<html><h4> $_[0] </h4>";
 7 }
 8
 9 sub start_table{
10 print "<table border=2><tr><td>";
11 }
12
13 sub end_table{
14 print "</td><tr></table>";
15 }
16
17 sub showvalue{
18 print "<li>Metal is $_[0]";
19 }
20
21 sub docfoot{
22 print "</html>\n";
23 }
24
25 1;
```

Calling Library Subroutines

In order for a Perl script to use a library the name of the library must be defined at the start of the script using the Perl "require" keyword.

The example below first defines that the script can use the library described on the facing page called "subs.lib".

The subroutines are then called in the usual way.

 Notice that the keyword is "require", and not "requires".

```
Edit     Run

 1  #!/usr/bin/perl
 2
 3  require "subs.lib";
 4
 5  &mimetype;
 6  &dochead("Subroutines Library");
 7  &start_table;
 8  &showvalue("Gold");
 9  &showvalue("Silver");
10  &showvalue("Bronze");
11  &end_table;
12  print "<li>A line from the script";
13  &docfoot;
```

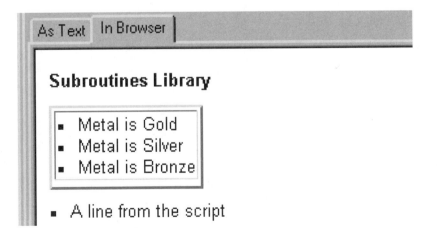

As Text   In Browser

Subroutines Library

- Metal is Gold
- Metal is Silver
- Metal is Bronze

- A line from the script

Returning Value

The Perl "return" keyword is used in subroutines to return a final value to the caller of that subroutine.

In the example on this page the subroutine caller passes two integer values as arguments to the subroutine. These integers are stored in the special underscore array.

The subroutine executes its code statements then the final value is returned to the caller using the "return" keyword.

This returned value is assigned to a scalar, then displayed.

*Unless specified with the "return" keyword, the default return value is that of the final expression evaluated in the statement block. So using "sub calc{ $_[0] * $_[1] }" could replace the subroutine in this example.*

Edit	Run

```perl
 1  #!/usr/bin/perl
 2
 3  $number=5;
 4  $multiplier=100;
 5  $result=calc($number,$multiplier);
 6
 7  print "content-type: text/html\n\n";
 8  print "<html>";
 9  print "<h4>Return Sub Value</h4>";
10  print "The result is $result";
11  print "</html>";
12
13  sub calc{
14  $sum= $_[0] * $_[1];
15  return $sum;
16  }
```

As Text	In Browser

Return Sub Value

The result is 500

Perl Functions

This chapter illustrates by how intrinsic Perl functions are useful in CGI scripting. Time and currency formatting are demonstrated along with random number generation. Also further examples are given of other useful functions.

Covers

Chapter Eight

Random Generator

The Perl "rand" function takes a single numeric argument and returns a random floating number between zero and the value of its argument.

The random number in the example will be between zero and 10, but not equal to or greater than 10.

The Perl "int" function gets the integer part of the floating number by truncating the number at the decimal point.

The example loop fills an array with six random numbers. By adding 1 to the returned integer the range will be between 1 and 49 inclusive.

| Edit | Run |

```perl
1  #!/usr/bin/perl
2
3  $num=rand(10);
4  $int=int($num);
5
6  for($i=0; $i<6; $i++){
7  $seq[$i]=int(rand(49))+1;
8  }
9
10 print "Content-type: text/html\n\n";
11 print "<html>";
12 print "<b>Random Numbers</b><br>";
13 print "<li>0-9 random is $num";
14 print "<li>Integer part is $int";
15 print "<li>Sequence is @seq";
16 print "</html>";
```

| As Text | In Browser |

Random Numbers
- 0-9 random is 8.66363525390625
- Integer part is 8
- Sequence is 44 5 36 21 49 32

Random Floats

The Perl "int" function can also be useful to truncate random numbers if shorter floating numbers are required.

The example below creates a floating number between zero and 50, then truncates it to two decimal places.

The random number is multiplied by 100 and the rest of the number is removed at the decimal point.

Dividing this truncated value by 100 leaves a floating number to two decimal places.

Random numbers can be useful to generate web page banners in a random manner.

```
Edit    Run

  1 #!/usr/bin/perl
  2
  3 $num=rand(50);
  4 $tmp=$num*100;
  5 $int=int($tmp);
  6 $flt=$int/100;
  7
  8 print "Content-type: text/html\n\n";
  9 print "<html>";
 10 print "<li>0-50 random = $num";
 11 print "<li>Multiplied x 100 = $tmp";
 12 print "<li>Integer part = $int";
 13 print "<li>Truncated float is $flt";
 14 print "</html>";
```

As Text | In Browser

- 0-50 random = 39.4271850585938
- Multiplied x 100 = 3942.71850585938
- Integer part = 3942
- Truncated float is 39.42

Data Formatting

In addition to the standard "print" function Perl can format the output data by using the "printf" function.

This function takes two arguments to specify the type of formatting required and the data to be formatted.

The second argument that specifies the data to be formatted can be a scalar variable.

The formatting type specified in the first argument always starts with a "%" character followed by the format required, and should be enclosed in quotes.

For instance, formatting to force data to have at least four integer digits is specified with "%4d". To ensure that leading zeroes are inserted this becomes "%04d".

The example below demonstrates the "printf" function formatting output. Also illustrated is the "sprintf" function that works in just the same way but is used when saving the formatted data to a scalar variable.

```
Edit    Run

 1  #!/usr/bin/perl
 2
 3  $savedformatted=sprintf("%04d",8);
 4
 5  print "Content-type: text/html\n\n";
 6  print "<html>";
 7  print "<li>Direct Formatted Output:";
 8  printf("%04d",256);
 9  print "<li>Saved Formatted Output:";
10  print "$savedformatted";
11  print "</html>";
```

```
As Text  In Browser

    ■  Direct Formatted Output:0256
    ■  Saved Formatted Output:0008
```

Currency Format

The "printf" and "sprintf" functions introduced on the facing page are commonly used to format currency sums.

Floating-point numbers can be formatted to force data to contain a specific number of decimal places.

These will be filled with zeroes where needed.

For instance, to force data to always have two decimal places formatting is specified with "%.2f".

This formatting is useful to add zeroes to the penny side of currency amounts so that "£7.50" does not become "£7.5".

In the following example the "sprintf" function saves a formatted currency sum to a scalar variable that is displayed by the Html code. Also the "printf" function is demonstrated directly formatting a currency output value.

```perl
#!/usr/bin/perl

$savedformatted=sprintf("%.2f",8.00);

print "Content-type: text/html\n\n";
print "<html>";
print "<li>Direct Formatted Sum: £";
printf("%.2f",7.50);
print "<li>Saved Formatted Sum: £";
print "$savedformatted";
print "</html>";
```

- Direct Formatted Sum: £7.50
- Saved Formatted Sum: £8.00

Handling Time

Perl has a number of useful features to handle time and date that are demonstrated in the example on the facing page.

The "time" keyword returns the current time in milliseconds from the system clock. This can be translated to local time and date information using the "localtime" function. Alternatively the "gmtime" function can translate it to date and time information at Greenwich Mean Time.

All eight components of either time function can be assigned to scalar variables using the syntax on lines 6 and 7.

The eight parts of the time data are always returned in this order so need to be assigned accordingly.

The example uses the "localtime" function returns but could equally have assigned the returns from the "gmtime" function if the data is required to be in GMT time format.

Most of the scalar variables will receive straightforward values but some need adjustment for meaningful use.

The $mon variable gets the month of the year starting at zero for January up to 11 for December. This value should be incremented for normal use so that January is month 1.

Similarly the $yday scalar gets the day number of the year again counting from zero at January 1st. So this value should also be incremented so the first day of the year is day 1.

The $year variable gets a count starting from 1900. So for the year 2003 the $year value is 103. To change this to the current year 1900 must be added.

The time information assigned to the $hour, $min and $sec scalars can be formatted to be always two digits using the Perl "sprintf" function. For instance, this would display a value of five minutes as "05" rather than just "5".

Two arguments are required by the "sprintf" function to specify the type of formatting, "%02d" for two digits, and the name of the scalar to be formatted.

If the time returned occurs during daylight savings time the $isdst scalar receives a true value of 1. Otherwise this variable will get a false value of zero.

The code on lines 6 & 7 would normally be on a single line, but is split here due to limited space.

| Edit | Run |

```perl
1  #!/usr/bin/perl
2
3  $servertime=localtime(time);
4  $gmt=gmtime(time);
5
6  ($sec,$min,$hour,$mday,$mon,$year,
7    $wday,$yday,$isdst)=localtime(time);
8
9  $mon++;   $yday++;   $year+=1900;
10 $hour = sprintf("%02d", $hour);
11 $min =   sprintf("%02d", $min);
12 $sec =   sprintf("%02d", $sec);
13 $ds = ($isdst==1)? "Yes":"No";
14
15 print <<"DOC";
16 content-type: text/html\n\n <html>
17 <li>Server Time: $servertime
18 <li>GMT Time: $gmt
19 <li>Date: $mday-$mon-$year
20 <li>Time: $hour:$min:$sec
21 <li>Daylight Saving: $ds
22 <li>Day of week: $wday
23 <li>Day of year: $yday        </html>
24 DOC
```

| As Text | In Browser |

- Server Time: Tue Oct 21 00:13:43 2003
- GMT Time: Mon Oct 20 23:13:43 2003
- Date: 21-10-2003
- Time: 00:13:43
- Daylight Saving: Yes
- Day of week: 2
- Day of year: 294

Chop String

The Perl "chop" function is used to remove the final character of a text string.

This function returns the character that has just been removed and shortens the original string.

In the example below the $str scalar is assigned an initial value that is displayed by the Html code. Then the "chop" function removes the last character and assigns it to a scalar.

The removed character and the newly shortened string are finally displayed in the Html code.

Edit	Run

```
 1 #!/usr/bin/perl
 2
 3 print "Content-type: text/html\n\n";
 4 print "<html><b>Chop...</b><br>";
 5
 6 $str = "PERL";
 7 print "<li>Original String: $str";
 8
 9 $char = chop( $str );
10 print "<li>Chopped Character: $char";
11 print "<li>Chopped String: $str";
12
13 print "</html>";
```

As Text	In Browser

Chop...
- Original String: PERL
- Chopped Character: L
- Chopped String: PER

Chomp New Lines

Not to be confused with the "chop" function, the Perl "chomp" function is used to safely remove only unseen characters from the end of a string.

Most commonly "chomp" removes the invisible new line characters that have been added by the user.

This example demonstrates the effect that "chomp" has on strings with and without ending new line characters:

It is advisable to "chomp" all user input to avoid problems with unseen characters like new lines.

```
Edit    Run

 1 #!/usr/bin/perl
 2
 3 print "Content-type: text/html\n\n";
 4 print "<html><b>Chomp...</b><br>";
 5 $regular = "CGI Script";
 6 $chompit=chomp($regular);
 7 print "<li>Chomp Regular: $regular";
 8 print "<li>Did Chomp: $chompit <hr>";
 9 $with_nl="CGI Script
10 ";
11 $chompit=chomp($with_nl);
12 print "<li>Chomp Newline: $with_nl";
13 print "<li>Did Chomp: $chompit";
14 print "</html>";
```

```
As Text    In Browser

Chomp...
  • Chomp Regular: CGI Script
  • Did Chomp: 0

  • Chomp Newline: CGI Script
  • Did Chomp: 1
```

Eval

The Perl "eval" function is useful to evaluate code statements and trap any errors they may contain.

If the evaluated statements contain a syntax error or a runtime error the "eval" function traps the error.

When errors are trapped a special Perl variable called "$@" is assigned an error message that describes the error.

When no errors are detected "eval" returns a true value of 1.

In the example below there is a deliberate syntax error in the statement that is to be evaluated.

The error message locates the error in the first line of the statement block of the first "eval" function in the script.

```
Edit | Run
 1 #!/usr/bin/perl
 2
 3 $num = 7;
 4
 5 eval("$num = ;");
 6
 7 if ($@ eq "")
 8 {
 9   print("eval() success");
10 }
11 else
12 {
13   print("eval() fail: $@");
14 }
```

As Text | In Browser

eval() fail: syntax error at (eval 1) line 1, at EOF

Warn And Die

When the "eval" function detects an error the user can receive a warning message using the Perl "warn" function.

This catches the error message from the special "$@" variable but allows the script to continue.

Alternatively the error can be caught with the Perl "die" function that will stop the script, as seen in this example:

The final warning in this example is not made because "die" has already stopped the script.

```
Edit    Run

   1  #!/usr/bin/perl
   2
   3  print "content-type:text/html\n\n";
   4  print "<html>DIE";
   5
   6  eval { alarm(100) };
   7  warn() if $@;
   8
   9  eval { alarm(100) };
  10  die() if $@;
  11
  12  eval { alarm(100) };
  13  warn() if $@;
  14
  15  print "</html>";
```

```
Messages                                          [x]

The Unsupported function alarm function is unimplemented
   at C:\WINDOWS\TEMP\DzTemp.pl line 6.
I...caught at C:\WINDOWS\TEMP\DzTemp.pl line 7.
The Unsupported function alarm function is unimplemented
   at C:\WINDOWS\TEMP\DzTemp.pl line 9.
I...propagated at C:\WINDOWS\TEMP\DzTemp.pl line 10.
```

Pack

The Perl "pack" function takes a list of values and converts them into a single string according the rules specified by its first argument.

Most usually this function will be converting to standard signed characters for which the rule is the letter "c".

The rule should be repeated for each item in the ensuing list that is to be converted.

This example demonstrates the "pack" function converting a list of ASCII character codes to a text string. Also a list of hexadecimal codes are converted to a text string:

 The "pack" function is very useful when handling encoded data from a web browser. See the form parser example on page 128 for details.

```perl
Edit    Run

 1  #!/usr/bin/perl
 2
 3  print "content-type:text/html\n\n";
 4  print "<html>";
 5
 6  $chrstr= pack("cccc",80,101,114,108);
 7
 8  $hexstr= pack("ccc",
 9          hex(0x8f),hex(0x93),hex(0x95));
10
11  print "<h2> $hexstr &amp;  $chrstr ";
12  print "in easy steps </h2>";
13
14  print "</html>";
```

```
As Text   In Browser

CGI & Perl in easy steps
```

Pattern Matching

This chapter introduces "Regular Expressions" to search through a string for a specified substring. The examples in this chapter show how to perform pattern matching and demonstrate how located matches can be manipulated in a variety of useful ways.

Covers

Chapter Nine

Match String

Perl syntax to search a string always requires the string, or its variable name, followed by the "=~" binding operator.

The search pattern is defined after the binding operator.

To find a match the "m" (for "match") identifier is used followed by the pattern to find enclosed by forward slashes.

Optionally the pattern definition can end with an "i" (for "ignore") quantifier to ignore case when searching. This is demonstrated in this example that searches for two matches:

There should be no spaces in the search pattern definition.

```
Edit    Run

  1 #!/usr/bin/perl
  2
  3 $str="She sang 'Shebang!' ";
  4 print "Content-type: text/html\n\n";
  5 print "<html><h4>String: $str</h4>";
  6
  7 if($str=~ m/she/i ){
  8 print "<li>Pattern 'she' matched";
  9 }else{
 10 print "<li>Pattern 'she' not found";
 11 }
 12
 13 $fnd=($str=~ m/line/i )?"Yes":"No";
 14 print "<li>Was 'line' found?: $fnd";
 15 print "</html>";
```

Notice how much more compact the code for the second search is on lines 13 and 14.

```
As Text   In Browser

String: She sang 'Shebang!'
  • Pattern 'she' matched
  • Was 'line' found?: No
```

View Match

There are three special Perl variables that can be used to manipulate text content following a successful match.

The actual string matched is contained in the "$&" ampersand variable.

All text in the searched string preceding the match is contained in the "$`" backtick variable. All text in the string after the match is contained in the "$'" apostrophe variable.

This example displays the contents of all three variables:

The "backtick" character key can normally be found above the "tab" key on a standard keyboard.

Edit	Run

```
 1 #!/usr/bin/perl
 2
 3 $str="She sang 'Shebang!' ";
 4 print "Content-type: text/html\n\n";
 5 print "<html><h4>String: $str</h4>";
 6
 7 $fnd=($str=~ m/sang/i )?"Yes":"No";
 8
 9 print "<li>Was 'sang' found?: $fnd";
10 print "<li>Text before match: $`";
11 print "<li>Text string matched: $&";
12 print "<li>Text after match: $'";
13 print "</html>";
```

As Text	In Browser

String: She sang 'Shebang!'

- Was 'sang' found?: Yes
- Text before match: She
- Text string matched: sang
- Text after match: 'Shebang!'

Substitute String

In addition to searching strings for a match to a specified pattern, Perl can replace the match when it has been found.

To replace a match the "s" (for "substitute") identifier is required when defining the search pattern.

The "s" search pattern in this example will only substitute the first match in the searched string.

This is followed by the pattern to find, enclosed by forward slashes as usual, then the string that is to replace the match.

A final forward slash terminates the replacement string and an "i" quantifier can be added if case is to be ignored.

The search pattern should not contain any spaces unless they form part of the pattern itself.

In this example the script searches the original string for the "bang" pattern that it replaces with the new specified text:

The "s" search is used to substitute spaces for the "+" character in the Form Parser script that is on page 128.

```
Edit   Run

 1 #!/usr/bin/perl
 2
 3 $str="She sang 'Shebang!!' ";
 4 print "Content-type: text/html\n\n";
 5 print "<html>";
 6 print "<h4>Original: $str</h4>";
 7
 8 $str=~ s/bang/DooBeDooBeDoo/i;
 9
10 print "<h4>Substitute: $str</h4>";
11 print "</html>";
```

```
As Text   In Browser

Original: She sang 'Shebang!'

Substitute: She sang 'SheDooBeDooBeDoo!'
```

Split Pattern

The Perl "split" function defines a search pattern as its first argument to specify at which point the string should be split.

A second argument specifies the name of the string to be searched and split.

The multiple separated strings can then be assigned to an array variable.

In this example a string is split at the common comma delimiter. The separated strings are stored in an array then a loop writes the content of each element to the Html code.

The "split" function is used to separate form data in the Form Parser script on page 128.

```perl
1  #!/usr/bin/perl
2
3  $abc="Alpha,Bravo,Charlie";
4  print "Content-type: text/html\n\n";
5  print "<html>";
6  print "<h4>Original: $abc</h4>";
7
8  @letters= split(/,/ ,$abc);
9
10 foreach $letter (@letters){
11 print "<li>$letter";
12 }
13 print "</html>";
```

As Text | **In Browser**

Original: Alpha,Bravo,Charlie
- Alpha
- Bravo
- Charlie

Translate

As an alternative to specifying a string to match in a search pattern definition a group of characters may be specified.

This is known as a "class" of characters and the character class is defined between square brackets.

The "tr" search pattern will translate all the matches within the string.

For example a class [1-5] would match all numbers in the range of 1 to 5 inclusive within a searched string.

Multiple ranges can be specified so the class [a-zA-Z] would match all uppercase and lowercase alphabet characters.

The example below uses the "tr" (for "translate") search pattern and the class [a-z] to match all lowercase characters.

In this case they are translated into uppercase characters by specifying the [A-Z] class as the new text.

The "tr" search is used to translate from hexadecimal in the Form Parser script on page 128.

Edit	Run

```
1  #!/usr/bin/perl
2
3  $str="She sang 'Shebang!!' ";
4  print "Content-type: text/html\n\n";
5  print "<html>";
6  print "<h4>Original: $str</h4>";
7
8  $str=~ tr/[a-z]/[A-Z]/;
9
10 print "<h4>Translated: $str</h4>";
11 print "</html>";
```

As Text	In Browser

Original: She sang 'Shebang!'

Translated: SHE SANG 'SHEBANG!'

Character Classes

The shorthand versions of frequently used character classes are listed in the table below and the example that follows demonstrates one of these in action.

The caret symbol (^) is used to mean a boolean "not".

Class	Equivalent	Match
\w	[a-zA-Z0-9_]	All letters, digits and underscores
\W	[^a-zA-Z0-9_]	Any characters other than letters, digits or underscores
\d	[0-9]	All digits
\D	[^0-9]	All characters except digits
\s	[\n\t\r\f]	All spaces, new lines, tabs, carriage returns and form feeds
\S	[^\n\t\r\f]	All characters except spaces, new lines, tabs, returns and form feeds

Remember that character class shorthands still need to be enclosed inside the square brackets.

```
Edit   Run

1 #!/usr/bin/perl
2
3 $str="CGI & Perl in easy steps";
4 print "Content-type: text/html\n\n";
5 print "<html><b>String: $str</b>";
6 if($str=~m/[\w]/){
7 print "<li>Letters found"}
8 print "</html>";
```

As Text | In Browser

String: CGI & Perl in easy steps
• Letters found

Inclusive Groups

Pattern matching can be used to determine the direction of a script by conditional branching for seeking included digits.

A search pattern is defined and if a match is found to be included in the searched string the script will follow an affirmative route.

In the example below the search pattern is defined as any digit in the range of zero to 4.

If the search matches any digit in the range 0-4 then the first statement in the statement block will be executed.

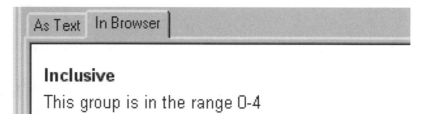

```
Edit   Run

    1 #!/usr/bin/perl
    2
    3 $str="Group 3";
    4
    5 print "Content-type: text/html\n\n";
    6 print "<html><h4>Inclusive</h4>";
    7 print "This group is in the range";
    8
    9 if( $str=~ m/[0-4]/ ){
   10 print " 0-4";
   11 }else{
   12 print " 5-9";
   13 }
   14
   15 print "</html>";
```

```
As Text  In Browser

Inclusive
This group is in the range 0-4
```

Exclusive Groups

Conditional branching can be performed with pattern matching by searching for excluded digits.

A search pattern is defined and if a match is found to be excluded from the searched string the script will follow a negative route.

In the following example the search pattern is defined as any digit not in the range of zero to 4.

If the search does not match a digit in the range 0-4 then the second statement in the statement block will be executed.

The caret symbol (^) is used as a boolean NOT operator.

```
Edit   Run

 1 #!/usr/bin/perl
 2
 3 $str="Group 3";
 4
 5 print "Content-type: text/html\n\n";
 6 print "<html><h4>Exclusive</h4>";
 7 print "This group is in the range";
 8
 9 if( $str=~ m/^[0-4]/ ){
10 print " 5-9";
11 }else{
12 print " 0-4";
13 }
14
15 print "</html>";
```

```
As Text   In Browser

Exclusive
This group is in the range 0-4
```

Limited Matching

In order to limit the matches to be only an exact match, qualifiers can be added to the search pattern definition.

The example below adds a caret symbol " ^ " in front of the search pattern. The search will then only match if the pattern appears at the start of the searched string.

Also the example adds a dollar symbol "$" after the search pattern. This ensures that the search will only match if the pattern appears at the end of the searched string.

If the example only added the caret qualifier "Hammer" would match. If the example only added the dollar qualifier "Wham" would match.

```
Edit   Run

 1 #!/usr/bin/perl
 2
 3 $ham="Ham"; $wham="Wham";
 4 $hammer="Hammer";
 5 $ok="Matched"; $no="No Match";
 6
 7 print "Content-type: text/html\n\n";
 8 print "<html><h4>Limited Match</h4>";
 9 $res=($ham=~ m/^Ham$/i)? $ok : $no;
10 {print "<li>$ham : $res"}
11 $res=($wham=~ m/^Ham$/i)? $ok : $no;
12 {print "<li>$wham : $res"}
13 $res=($hammer=~ m/^Ham$/i)? $ok:$no;
14 {print "<li>$hammer : $res"}
15 print "</html>";
```

```
As Text   In Browser

Limited Match
 • Ham : Matched
 • Wham : No Match
 • Hammer : No Match
```

Optional Matching

Using a "?" qualifier after a search pattern enables the search to report a match whether the match is made or not.

It is important to note that the "?" qualifier will normally only work with the single character immediately before it.

The search pattern must be enclosed in brackets for the "?" qualifier to work with the whole pattern.

This example matches both searches even though the pattern in the second search is not actually in the searched string:

```perl
Edit    Run

 1 #!/usr/bin/perl
 2
 3 $str="She sang 'Shebang!'";
 4 $ok= "Matched";
 5 $no= "No Match";
 6
 7 print "Content-type: text/html\n\n";
 8 print "<html>";
 9 print "<h4>Optional Match</h4>";
10 print "<li>String: $str";
11 $res=($str=~ m/(she)?/i)? $ok : $no;
12 {print "<li>She : $res"}
13 $res=($str=~ m/(shout)?/i)? $ok:$no;
14 {print "<li>Shout : $res"}
15 print "</html>";
```

```
As Text   In Browser

Optional Match
  • String: She sang 'Shebang!'
  • She : Matched
  • Shout : Matched
```

Minimum Match

In cases where multiple matches are possible the "+" qualifier can be added after a search pattern to specify that the search must make at least one match.

This example assigns the search pattern to a variable then calls a subroutine to make the search and display the results.

```
Edit    Run

 1 #!/usr/bin/perl
 2
 3 $str="She sang 'Shebang!'";
 4 print "Content-type: text/html\n\n";
 5 print "<html>";
 6 print "<h4>Match At Least Once</h4>";
 7 print "<li>String: $str";
 8 $exp="She";
 9 &report;
10 $exp="Shout";
11 &report;
12 print "</html>";
13
14 sub report(){
15 $res=($str=~ m/($exp)+/);
16 print "<li>$exp : Found"  if $res==1;
17 print "<li>$exp : Failed" if $res!=1;
18 }
```

The qualifier will only apply to the single character preceding it unless the regular expression is enclosed in brackets.

```
As Text   In Browser

Match At Least Once
  • String: She sang 'Shebang!'
  • She : Found
  • Shout : Failed
```

Alternative Match

A search definition can specify more than one pattern to search for by separating each pattern with the "|" operator.

The first search in the example below matches the second specified pattern.

The second search matches neither of its specified patterns.

This example numbers each search from a counter variable that has been initialized at the beginning of the script then is incremented by each search.

Nested strings must have their quotes escaped to avoid the string being prematurely terminated.

Edit	Run

```perl
1  #!/usr/bin/perl
2
3  $str="She sang 'Shebang!'"; $i=1;
4  print "Content-type: text/html\n\n";
5  print "<html>";
6  print "<h4>Alternative Matches</h4>";
7  print "<li>String: $str";
8  $res=($str=~ m/Shout|She/); &report;
9  $res=($str=~ m/Shout|Sham/); &report;
10 print "</html>";
11
12 sub report(){
13 if ($res == 1){
14 print "<li>Search $i : \"$&\" Found";
15 }else{
16 print "<li>Search $i : No Matches";}
17 $i++;
18 }
```

As Text	In Browser

Alternative Matches

- String: She sang 'Shebang!'
- Search 1 : 'She' Found
- Search 2 : No Matches

Multiple Matches

Adding a "g" (for "global") qualifier to the end of the search definition allows multiple matches to be stored in an array.

This example searches for three patterns then assigns the matches to an array.

Finally a loop displays the contents of each element.

The search in this example finds two instances of "She" in the searched string so each instance is assigned to an array element.

```
Edit    Run

 1  #!/usr/bin/perl
 2
 3  $str="She sang 'Shebang!'";
 4
 5  print "Content-type: text/html\n\n";
 6  print "<html>";
 7  print "<h4>Multiple Matches</h4>";
 8  print "<li>String: $str";
 9
10  @match=($str=~ m/shout|she|bang/ig);
11  $length=@match;
12
13  for($i=0; $i<$length; $i++){
14  print "<li>Matched : $match[$i]";
15  }
16
17  print "</html>";
```

```
As Text   In Browser

Multiple Matches
 • String: She sang 'Shebang!'
 • Matched : She
 • Matched : She
 • Matched : bang
```

CGI From Web Pages

This exciting chapter demonstrates how web pages can interact with Perl scripts using CGI. Different methods of sending data from the browser to the server are demonstrated. The form parser is detailed in full and examples are given in sending data back to the browser.

Covers

Chapter Ten

Hyperlinks To CGI

The exciting use of Perl in CGI scripts creates a two-way exchange between the HTML code on the browser page and the Perl code on the web server.

Refer to page 16 for details on setting up a local intranet environment with the Xitami web server.

To demonstrate this exchange all further examples in this book use the Xitami web server as a local intranet.

This allows the browser to communicate with the Xitami web server on the same computer using the HTTP protocol.

If the "auto-start" option was selected during the Xitami installation process then the web server automatically starts when the operating system boots up. Alternatively it can be manually started with the Xitami icon on the start menu.

A small green Xitami icon is displayed in the system tray to indicate that the Xitami web server is running.

All CGI scripts on the web server must be placed in the server's "cgi-bin" directory. The location on the local computer with the Xitami server is at C:\Xitami\cgi-bin.

The simplest way to communicate with a CGI script is via a hyperlink in the HTML code. When the user follows that link the CGI script will be called and the Perl code will run.

The URL syntax for hyperlinks to CGI scripts follows the standard pattern of protocol, domain name and file name:

```
http://localhost/cgi-bin/hello.cgi
```

The intranet domain name can also be the computer name that is found under the "Identification" tab from the "Network" icon in Control Panel.

With the local intranet, the domain is called "localhost".

The URL above addresses a file called "hello.cgi" that is in the "cgi-bin" folder on the local intranet server.

This URL address can be used in a HTML document to run the CGI script when the user clicks a hyperlink. The URL is simply made the target of the link in much the same way that a link can target another HTML page:

```
<a href="http://localhost/cgi-bin/hello.cgi">Click</a>
```

The hyperlink could appear in the HTML code as shown below together with how it may appear in the web browser:

```
<html>
<body>
<a href="http://localhost/cgi-bin/hello.cgi">Click</a>
</body>
</html>
```

The example "hello.cgi" script contains the following Perl code that produces the web browser output shown below:

The shebang line must show the path to the Perl interpreter on the host system at C:/Perl/bin/perl.

```
#!C:/Perl/bin/perl

print "Content-type: text/html\n\n";
print "<html><h1>Hello World</h1></html>";
```

Using Environment Variables

Each time a web browser communicates with a web server it passes certain data about itself to the server.

This data is stored by the server as "environment variables" in a special hash variable called %ENV.

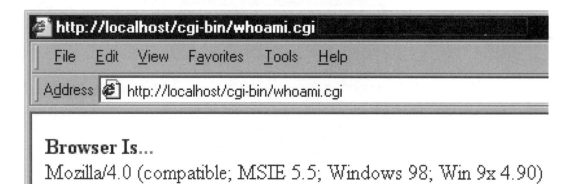

Uppercase characters are always used when addressing the environment variables.

The individual environment variable values can be accessed from a CGI Perl script by addressing their %ENV hash keys.

A list of typical useful environment variables appears on the inside front cover of this book.

The environment variables will change depending on the type of server software and the data sent from the browser.

It is sometimes useful for the CGI script to establish the browser being used to call the script. This information is available in environment variable "HTTP_USER_AGENT".

```
<a href="http://localhost/cgi-bin/whoami.cgi">Click</a>
```

The hyperlink in the HTML code above calls the following script to display browser details. The output describes Internet Explorer 5.5 running on a Windows ME platform:

```
#!C:/Perl/bin/perl

print "Content-type: text/html\n\n";
print "<html><b>Browser Is...</b></br>";
print "$ENV{'HTTP_USER_AGENT'} </html>";
```

http://localhost/cgi-bin/whoami.cgi

File   Edit   View   Favorites   Tools   Help

Address http://localhost/cgi-bin/whoami.cgi

Browser Is...
Mozilla/4.0 (compatible; MSIE 5.5; Windows 98; Win 9x 4.90)

See All Environment Variables

To see all the environment variables that have been set the following script loops through all the variables and writes their name and value in a HTML table:

```
#!C:/Perl/bin/perl

print "content-type:text/html\n\n";
print "<html>";
print "<table cellspacing=1 border=1>";

foreach $env_var (keys %ENV){
print "<tr><td bgcolor='silver'>$env_var</td>";
print "<td>$ENV{$env_var}</td></tr>";
}

print "</table>";
print "</html>";
```

A small part of the full table output is illustrated below:

See page 182 for examples of how to use the HTTP_REFERER variable.

http://localhost/cgi-bin/allenvvars.cgi	
File Edit View Favorites Tools Help	
Address 🥑 http://localhost/cgi-bin/allenvvars.cgi	
HTTP_ACCEPT_LANGUAGE	en-us
CGI_STDOUT	C:\DOS\pipe0030.cgo
SERVER_VERSION	2.4d6
CGI_URL	/cgi-bin
SCRIPT_PATH	cgi-bin
HTTP_USER_AGENT	Mozilla/4.0 (compatible
HTTP_ACCEPT	*/*
HTTP_HOST	localhost
GATEWAY_INTERFACE	CGI/1.1

GET Data From Hyperlinks

In addition to simply calling CGI scripts from an HTML document hyperlinks can be used to pass information from the web browser to the CGI script on the web server.

The data to be sent to the script is appended to the URL of the CGI script as a pair with the syntax "key=value".

This pair must be preceded by a question mark so the complete syntax looks like this:

```
protocol://domain_name/file_name?key=value
```

The other method to send data is "POST" which should be used to submit data from HTML forms. The "GET" method is not recommended for use with HTML forms.

Sending data this way uses a transmission method called "GET" and this method is recorded in an environment variable called "$ENV{'REQUEST_METHOD'}".

When the "GET" method is used the data is stored in an environment variable called "$ENV{'QUERY_STRING'}".

The example below sends a single key/value pair to a CGI script that displays the "$ENV{'REQUEST_METHOD'}" and "$ENV{'QUERY_STRING'}" environment variables.

Address	http://localhost/cgi-bin/hi.cgi?name=mike

```
#!C:/Perl/bin/perl
print "Content-type: text/html\n\n";
print "<html><li>Query String: $ENV{'QUERY_STRING'}";
print "<li>Method Used: $ENV{'REQUEST_METHOD'}</html>";
```

http://localhost/cgi-bin/hi.cgi?name=mike

File	Edit	View	Favorites	Tools	Help

Address	http://localhost/cgi-bin/hi.cgi?name=mike

- Query String: name=mike
- Method Used: GET

...cont'd

The example CGI scripts on these pages are called by simply typing the URL in the browser's address bar.

The "$ENV{'REQUEST_METHOD'}" can be tested by the CGI script to see if the "GET" method has been used to send data to the script.

If the test returns true the "$ENV{'QUERY_STRING'}" environment variable must contain data from the browser.

The key and value are contained in the data on either side of a "=" symbol. This can be used by the Perl "split" function to assign the separate key and value to individual variables.

The following example sends a single key/value pair to a CGI script that tests for the "GET" method then splits the key/value data around the "=" symbol.

The separated data is assigned to individual variables which are subsequently displayed in the HTML code.

Address   http://localhost/cgi-bin/split.cgi?name=mike

Escape nested quotes with a preceding backslash.

```
#!C:/Perl/bin/perl
print "Content-type: text/html\n\n";
print "<html>";
if( $ENV{"REQUEST_METHOD"} eq "GET"){
($key, $value) = split(/=/, $ENV{"QUERY_STRING"} );
}
print "<li>Key Is \" $key \" ";
print "<li>Value Is \" $value \" ";
print "</html>";
```

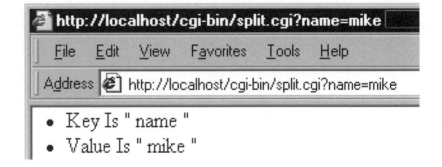

http://localhost/cgi-bin/split.cgi?name=mike

File   Edit   View   Favorites   Tools   Help

Address   http://localhost/cgi-bin/split.cgi?name=mike

- Key Is " name "
- Value Is " mike "

GET Multiple Data From Links

Multiple key/value pairs can be sent to the web server from a hyperlink in a web browser. The key/value pairs must be separated by a "&" character so the syntax looks like this:

```
protocol://domain_name/file_name?key=value&key=value
```

The "$ENV{'QUERY_STRING'}" environment variable contains all the key/value data complete with "&" separators.

Each pair can be separated, using the "split" function around the "&" separators, and placed into an array so that each array element stores one complete key/value pair.

Subsequently each pair can be split into key and value data using the "split" function around the "=" character.

This example separates two key/value pairs from the URL "http://localhost/cgi-bin/many.cgi?name=mike&sex=male":

Refer back to page 78 for more on the "foreach" loop.

```perl
#!C:/Perl/bin/perl
print "Content-type: text/html\n\n";
print "<html>";
if( $ENV{"REQUEST_METHOD"} eq "GET"){
@pairs = split(/&/, $ENV{"QUERY_STRING"});
}
foreach $pair (@pairs){
($key, $value) = split(/=/, $pair );
print "<li>Key: $key - Value: $value";
}
print "</html>";
```

Parsing GET Data

When data is sent from the browser to the server all spaces contained in the data are converted to "+" symbols.

Also all non-numeric special characters are converted into their hexadecimal equivalent preceded by a "%" symbol.

For more on the translate form of pattern matching see page 106.

The receiving CGI script needs to convert both of these back into their more usual format when parsing the data.

Spaces using "+" can be translated back using this code:

```
$key =~ tr/+/ /;
$value =~ tr/+/ /;
```

For more on the substitute form of pattern matching see page 104.

Any special non-alphanumeric characters can be converted back from hexadecimal format to their usual format like this:

```
$key =~ s/%(..)/pack("c",hex($1))/eg;
$value =~ s/%(..)/pack("c",hex($1))/eg;
```

In this example these lines of code are added to the previous script to ensure that the data output appears correctly:

For more on the pack function see the example on page 100.

```
foreach $pair (@pairs){
($key, $value) = split(/=/, $pair );

$key =~ tr/+/ /; $key =~ s/%(..)/pack("c",hex($1))/eg;
$value=~ tr/+/ /;$value =~ s/%(..)/pack("c",hex($1))/eg;

print "<li>Key: $key - Value: $value";
}
```

POST Data From Forms

A HTML form will typically be submitted to a CGI script on the server when the user pushes the form's submit button.

The method for transmitting the form data is specified in the HTML form as either "GET" or "POST".

When the "GET" method is used to submit the form, data is tacked onto the URL using the familiar "key=value" syntax.

However, many servers limit the amount of data that can be received by the "GET" method so it is recommended that HTML forms should always use the "POST" method.

This is how a simple HTML form might look to provide a single text field for the user to enter text and a submit button to send the text to the CGI script on the server:

The "action" attribute of the form element is used to specify the address of the desired CGI script.

```
<html>
<head>
<title>Send Text Form</title>
</head>
<body>
<form method="POST"
action="http://localhost/cgi-bin/showtext.cgi">
<input type="text" name="text1" size="25">
<input type="submit" value="Send Text">
</form>
<body>
</html>
```

Send Text Form

File   Edit   View   Favorites   Tools   Help

Address   C:\WINDOWS\Desktop\sendtext.html

Perl   Send Text

When the "POST" method is used, the environment variable "$ENV{'REQUEST_METHOD'}" is set to "POST" and the environment variable "$ENV{'CONTENT_LENGTH'}" is set to an integer value representing the datalength.

The actual form data is stored at a "standard input" location on the server called "STDIN" that can be read from a script.

Perl's "read" function can assign the form data from the "STDIN" location to a scalar variable by specifying the name of the scalar and the form data length to be assigned.

In the example below, the form data illustrated on the facing page is assigned to a scalar variable by the "read" function.

The form data is displayed in the HTML output together with both of the environment variable values.

It is common practice to name the receiving scalar variable "$buffer" when reading from the "STDIN" location.

```perl
#!C:/Perl/bin/perl
print "Content-type: text/html\n\n";
print "<html>";
if( $ENV{'REQUEST_METHOD'} eq 'POST'){
read(STDIN, $buffer, $ENV{'CONTENT_LENGTH'});
}
print "<li>For Data: $buffer";
print "<li>Submission Method: $ENV{'REQUEST_METHOD'}";
print "<li>Content Length: $ENV{'CONTENT_LENGTH'}";
print "</html>";
```

http://localhost/cgi-bin/showtext.cgi

File Edit View Favorites Tools Help

Address http://localhost/cgi-bin/showtext.cgi

- For Data: text1=Perl
- Submission Method: POST
- Content Length: 10

POST Multiple Data From Forms

Multiple key/value pairs that are submitted by a form can be split around their "&" delimiters. Each pair can then be assigned to the elements of an array. Individual keys and values can be accessed by further splitting each pair around their "=" separator as usual.

The example below sends two key/value pairs to the CGI script which separates them and displays each component:

The key/value pairs are handled in just the same way as seen in the GET example on page 122.

```perl
#!C:/Perl/bin/perl
print "Content-type: text/html\n\n<html>";
if( $ENV{'REQUEST_METHOD'} eq 'POST'){
read(STDIN, $buffer, $ENV{'CONTENT_LENGTH'});
@pairs = split(/&/, $buffer);
}
foreach $pair (@pairs){
($key, $value) = split(/=/, $pair );
print "<li>Key: $key - Value: $value";
}
print "</html>";
```

The value of the text2 input illustrates the conversion of spaces to "+" symbols and the ampersand character to hexadecimal.

Parsing POST Data

The translation of "+" space symbols and hexadecimal characters is handled in just the same way as the earlier GET example on page 123.

When data is sent from the browser to the server all spaces contained in the data are converted to "+" symbols.

Also all non-numeric special characters are converted into their hexadecimal equivalent preceded by a "%" symbol.

The example on the facing page illustrates these conversions.

In order to convert both of these back to their usual format the script below adds parsing routines to the earlier code.

The "+" symbols spaces are now translated to spaces and regular characters are substituted for hexadecimal characters.

See page 106 for translate. See page 104 for substitute. See page 100 for the pack function.

```perl
#!C:/Perl/bin/perl
print "Content-type: text/html\n\n<html>";
if( $ENV{'REQUEST_METHOD'} eq 'POST'){
read(STDIN, $buffer, $ENV{'CONTENT_LENGTH'});
@pairs = split(/&/, $buffer);
}
foreach $pair (@pairs){
($key, $value) = split(/=/, $pair );

$key =~ tr/+/ /;
$value =~ tr/+/ /;
$key =~ s/%(..)/pack("c", hex($1))/eg;
$value =~ s/%(..)/pack("c", hex($1))/eg;

print "<li>Key: $key - Value: $value";
}
print "</html>";
```

http://localhost/cgi-bin/showdata2.cgi

File   Edit   View   Favorites   Tools   Help

Address   http://localhost/cgi-bin/showdata2.cgi

- Key: text1 - Value: Mike
- Key: text2 - Value: CGI & Perl

The Form Parser

Handling HTML forms with CGI scripts is so common that it is convenient to create a standard library file containing the code to carry out the form parsing routines.

The form parser below combines the code to handle both "GET" and "POST" form submission methods. It adds a further section to allow for forms that are submitted with extra data appended to the URL.

Library files have no shebang line and must end with a 1. For more details on library files see page 86.

This form parser will ignore Server-Side Includes and will display a message if GET or POST methods are not used.

```perl
sub parseform{

if ($ENV{'REQUEST_METHOD'} eq 'GET') {
@pairs = split(/&/, $ENV{'QUERY_STRING'});
}
elsif ($ENV{'REQUEST_METHOD'} eq 'POST') {
read (STDIN, $buffer, $ENV{'CONTENT_LENGTH'});
@pairs = split(/&/, $buffer);
if ($ENV{'QUERY_STRING'}) {
@getpairs =split(/&/, $ENV{'QUERY_STRING'});
push(@pairs,@getpairs);    }
}
else {
print "content-type:text/html\n\n";
print "Unrecognized Request Method - Use GET or POST.";
}

foreach $pair (@pairs) {
($key, $value) = split(/=/, $pair);
$key =~ tr/+/ /;
$key =~ s/%(..)/pack("c", hex($1))/eg;
$value =~ tr/+/ /;
$value =~ s/%(..)/pack("c", hex($1))/eg;
$value =~s/<!--(.|\n)*-->//g;   # ignore SSI

if ($formdata{$key}) {
$formdata{$key} .= ", $value";
}
else { $formdata{$key} = $value; }
}
}

1;
```

The form parser creates a hash called "%formdata" in which all the parsed keys and their values are stored. Multiple values for the same key are stored as a comma-delimited list.

In order for the library file to be accessible to other CGI scripts it must be placed in the server's cgi-bin directory.

The example below uses the form parser to process the illustrated HTML form and displays the input values:

Enter Three Colours

File   Edit   View   Favorites   Tools   Help

Address   C:\WINDOWS\Desktop\colours.html

1: Red   2: Green   3: Blue   Send

The form parser is called "formparser.lib" and associated with the CGI script using the "require" keyword. The parseform subroutine is called by the "&parseform;" instruction.

```perl
#!C:/Perl/bin/perl

require "formparser.lib";
&parseform;

print "Content-type: text/html\n\n <html>";
print "You entered these colours: ";
print "$formdata{'colour1'}, ";
print "$formdata{'colour2'} ";
print "and $formdata{'colour3'}    </html>";
```

http://localhost/cgi-bin/colours.cgi

File   Edit   View   Favorites   Tools   Help

Address   http://localhost/cgi-bin/colours.cgi

You entered these colours: Red, Green and Blue

Output All Parsed Form Data

This example loops through the "formdata" hash, created by the form parser, to show all the parsed keys and values:

```
#!C:/Perl/bin/perl
require "formparser.lib";
&parseform;
print "Content-type: text/html\n\n<html>";
foreach $key (keys %formdata){
print "<li>Key: $key - Value: $formdata{$key}"; }
print "</html>";
```

- Key: author - Value: Mike McGrath
- Key: topic - Value: JavaScript
- Key: price - Value: £9.99

Working With Files

This chapter illustrates how Perl CGI scripts can read and write text files on the server. There are demonstrations of how these features can be used to create a simple hit counter and guest book.

Covers

Chapter Eleven

Read From A Text File

The Perl "open" and "close" functions are used to both read from, and write to, text files on the server.

The "open" function creates a "text stream" containing the contents of the first line of characters in the text file.

Remember to close the text stream after assigning the contents.

A "file handle" label must be given, as the first argument to the "open" function, to be used to refer to the text stream.

The second argument specifies the name of the text file to be opened. If the text file is not in the cgi-bin directory the full path to the text file should be stated.

A "<" character must immediately precede the file name or path to indicate that the text file is to be read.

This example opens a text file in the cgi-bin directory then assigns the first line to a scalar for display in the output.

📄 textfile.txt

CGI & Perl in easy steps

Notice the syntax used with the label when assigning to text stream – the file handle label must be enclosed in angle brackets.

```
#!C:/Perl/bin/perl

open(TXT, "<textfile.txt");
$text = <TXT>;
close(TXT);

print "content-type:text/html\n\n <html>";
print "Text File Contents: $text   </html>";
```

Read All Text Lines

A text stream from an opened text file can store multiple lines of text when assigned to an array variable. Each array element contains a line of characters from the text file.

The example below uses the relative address of the text file in the "logs" folder to open the text stream.

All lines in the text stream are assigned to an array using the file handle label.

The "foreach" loop displays each line of text contained in the array elements when writing the HTML output.

📄 textfile.txt

```
CGI & Perl in easy steps
Written by Mike McGrath
From ComputerStep Books
```

Remember to close the text stream after assigning the contents.

```perl
#!C:/Perl/bin/perl

open(TXT, "<../logs/textfile.txt");
@text=<TXT>;
close(TXT);
print "content-type:text/html\n\n <html>";
foreach $line (@text){
print "$line <br>";
}
print "</html>";
```

http://localhost/cgi-bin/alltext.cgi

File   Edit   View   Favorites   Tools   Help

CGI & Perl in easy steps
Written by Mike McGrath
From ComputerStep Books

Write To A Text File

The Perl "open" function can be used to create a new text file or update an existing file by over-writing its contents.

First the Perl "open" function opens the existing text file or, if none exists, creates a new file with the specified name.

Always place text files in the cgi-bin folder to avoid confusion.

The "open" function takes two arguments to specify a file handle label for the text stream and the name of the text file.

A ">" character must immediately precede the file name to indicate that the function should write to the file.

The "print" function states the name of the file handle then the string to be written in the text file.

This can be repeated to add more content before the text stream is closed by the "close" function.

Here a new text file called "datafile.txt" is created then two lines of text are added before the text stream is closed:

```
#!C:/Perl/bin/perl

open(TXT, ">datafile.txt");
print TXT "Message From CGI Script:\n";
print TXT "File handling is easy with Perl";
close(TXT);
```

writetext.cgi   datafile.txt

cgi-bin

datafile.txt

```
Message From CGI Script:
File handling is easy with Perl
```

Hit Counter

A text file on the server can be used as a "hit-counter" that stores an integer value recording the number of times a web page has been opened.

This example reads the current count, then increments that value and saves the new count back in the text file. The new count is formatted to 5 digits then displayed in the output.

counter.txt

```
29
```

```perl
#!C:/Perl/bin/perl

open(COUNT, "<counter.txt");
$num = <COUNT>;
close(COUNT);

$num++;

open(COUNT, ">counter.txt");
print COUNT $num;
close(COUNT);

$num=sprintf("%05d",$num);

print "content-type:text/html\n\n  <html>";
print "You are visitor number $num </html>";
```

For more on formatting see the examples on page 92–93.

counter.txt

```
30
```

http://localhost/cgi-bin/shownum.cgi

File   Edit   View   Favorites   Tools   Help

You are visitor number 00030

Append To Existing Text File

The Perl "open" function can be used to add text to an existing text file by appending text to its current contents.

First the Perl "open" function opens the existing text file that is to be updated or creates a new file if none exists.

The "open" function takes two arguments to specify a file handle label for the text stream and the name of the text file.

The ">>" characters must immediately precede the file name to indicate that the function should append text.

The "print" function states the name of the file handle then the string to be appended to the text file.

This can be repeated to add more content before the text stream is closed by the "close" function.

Here an existing text file called "content.txt" is opened then more text is appended before the text stream is closed:

content.txt

```
Here is some text
```

Text will be appended immediately following any existing text.
Use "\n" to state new lines.

```
#!C:/Perl/bin/perl

open(TXT, ">>content.txt");

print TXT " and \nhere is some more text.";

print TXT "\nPerl appended this extra text.";

close(TXT);
```

content.txt

```
Here is some text and
here is some more text.
Perl appended this extra text.
```

Guest Messages

A simple guest book appends messages from a form to a text file which can then be read to display all the messages:

This form has two text inputs named "msg" and "from" whose names and values are submitted to the script as key/value pairs.

A form parser processes the submitted data which is then appended to a text file, as in the example on the previous page. All the text file content is then assigned to an array, as with the example on page 133.

```perl
#!C:/Perl/bin/perl

require "formparser.lib"; &parseform;

$txt= $formdata{'msg'};  $name=$formdata{'from'};

open(TXT, ">>messages.txt");
print TXT "Message: $txt - From $name \n";
close(TXT);

open(DATA, "<messages.txt");
@data = <DATA>;
close(DATA);

print "Content-type: text/html\n\n";
foreach $item(@data){ print "<li>$item"; }
print "</html>\n";
```

Exclusive File Access

When a text file has been opened by a script to read, write or append data it is essential, to avoid file errors, that no other script attempts to access that same text file concurrently.

The Perl "flock" function performs a "file lock" to ensure that the operation being performed on the text file will not be interrupted.

The "flock" function takes two arguments to specify the file handle label and a numeric indicator of the lock required. An indicator of "2" signifies that exclusive access should be granted to that instance of the script.

On completion of the operation with the text file the script should again call the "flock" function to release the file for access by other scripts. The releasing call must state the file handle label and an indicator of "8" as its two arguments.

This script uses the "flock" function when appending a date string to an existing text file:

When creating Perl CGI scripts on a platform not supporting "flock" include any flock calls in the script but comment them out with a '#' until the script is ready to be uploaded to the server.

```
#!C:/Perl/bin/perl

$gmt=gmtime(time);

open(NOW, ">datefile.txt");
flock(NOW, 2);
print NOW "$gmt";
flock(NOW, 8);
close(NOW);
```

To limit the length of time that the text file is inaccessible to other scripts only operations directly involving the text file should be performed while the file is locked.

For instance, in the example above the date is assigned to the variable before the file is locked.

The Perl "flock" function is supported on Unix and Windows NT platforms. It is not supported on other versions of Windows where scripts that use the "flock" function may not perform correctly.

Adding Error Messages

In the event that the anticipated file operation fails it is good to advise the user of the error.

When an error occurs Perl sets the special variable "$!" with a string describing that error.

A subroutine can be used to write the error message contained in the "$!" variable when an error occurs.

The Perl "exit" function stops any further execution of the script code after the error message has been written.

In the example below the script attempts to open a text file.

When the file is not found the error message contained in "$!" is passed to the subroutine for display to the user and the script is halted by "exit".

See page 84 for more on passing values to subroutines with "$_[0]".

```perl
#!C:/Perl/bin/perl

open(TXT, "<nosuch.txt") || &error($!);
@data= <TXT>;
close(TXT);

print "content-type:text/html\n\n <html>";
foreach $item(@data){
print "<li> $item";
}
print "</html>";

sub error{
print "content-type:text/html\n\n";
print "<html> <h3> Error: $_[0] </h3> </html>";
exit;
}
```

Renaming Files

The Perl "rename" function is useful both to rename and relocate files into other folders.

Two arguments are required with the "rename" function to specify the name of the old and new file names. If the file is not in the cgi-bin directory the absolute address is needed.

In the example below one file is simply renamed from "data.txt" to "newlog.txt". A second file is renamed from "log.txt" to "oldlog.txt" and simultaneously relocated to the "log" sub-folder in the cgi-bin directory. Finally a third file named "temp.txt" is just relocated to the "log" sub-folder while keeping the same file name.

The file URLs specified as the "rename" function arguments must be contained in quotes.

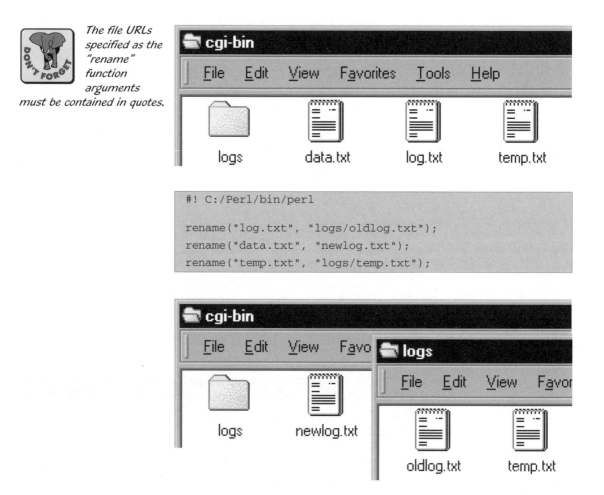

```
#! C:/Perl/bin/perl

rename("log.txt", "logs/oldlog.txt");
rename("data.txt", "newlog.txt");
rename("temp.txt", "logs/temp.txt");
```

Deleting Files

Files can be deleted from the server directories from within CGI scripts by utilising the Perl "unlink" function.

The "unlink" function takes a single argument that is the name of the file that is to be deleted.

If the file is not in the cgi-bin directory the absolute address is needed.

Multiple files to be deleted can be specified as a comma-delimited list forming the single argument to the function.

The following example builds on the example on the facing page to remove all three illustrated files.

The single file named "newlog.txt" is first deleted from the cgi-bin folder.

Then both files in the "logs" sub-folder are deleted in a single operation of the "unlink" function.

```
#! C:/Perl/bin/perl

unlink("newlog.txt");

unlink("logs/oldlog.txt","logs/temp.txt");
```

For details on how to delete the empty folder in this example see the "rmdir" function that is demonstrated on page 147.

To verify that the files no longer exist the script could test their file status using the "-e" Perl operator. This is part of a range of special operators that are described and demonstrated on the next page.

File Status

A file can be set with permissions to determine how it may be used. For instance, a file that is "read-only" does not permit Perl to write new content to it.

The status of a file and its permissions can be tested with a special set of Perl operators that are listed in this table:

Operator	Operation
-e	Does the file exist?
-d	Is the file a directory?
-r	Do the permissions allow the file to be read?
-w	Do the permissions allow writing to the file?
-x	Do the permissions allow the file to be executed?

For more on file permissions see page 148.

This example checks the status of a file called "log.txt":

```perl
#! C:/Perl/bin/perl

$e=(-e "log.txt") ? "Exists" : "Does Not Exist";
$d=(-d "log.txt") ? "Directory" : "Not A Directory";
$r=(-r "log.txt") ? "Readable" : "Not Readable";
$w=(-w "log.txt") ? "Writable" : "Not Writable";
$x=(-x "log.txt") ? "Executable" : "Not Executable";

print "content-type:text/html\n\n <html>";
print "log.txt status: $e - $d<br>$r - $w - $x </html>";
```

Handling Directories

This chapter illustrates how to work with files and directory structures. Creation and deletion of directories is demonstrated. File permissions are explained with examples of how they can be changed by Perl scripts.

Covers

Chapter Twelve

View Working Directory

The contents of a directory can be viewed in a similar manner to that used to read text files.

The current directory is addressed by "." while ".." addresses the next directory level up.

Perl's "opendir" function requires a file handle label and directory address to open the directory to be viewed.

The contents can be assigned to an array by the "readdir" function that specifies the file handle label as its argument.

Finally the directory text stream must be closed with the Perl "closedir" function and the file handle label.

This example views all files in the working cgi-bin directory and sorts them into alphabetical order:

```
#!C:/Perl/bin/perl

opendir(DIR, ".");
@files = readdir(DIR);
@files=sort(@files);
closedir(DIR);

print "content-type:text/html\n\n <html>";
foreach $file(@files){
print "$file - ";
}
print "</html>";
```

Notice that the contents of the directory that is viewed includes all system files.

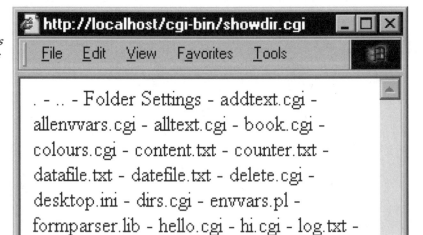

View Selected File Type

The Perl "grep" function can be used to restrict the files listed in a directory view to just one specific file type.

Two arguments are needed by the "grep" function.

The first argument specifies a pattern that is the file type and the second argument provides a full list of directory files.

Only when the "grep" function matches its search pattern, in the list of files, is that file assigned to an array element.

The example below searches for a match to the string ".txt" and assigns only correct matches to the files array:

Use a backslash to escape the "." period character in the search pattern.

```
#!C:/Perl/bin/perl

opendir(DIR, ".");
@files = grep( /\.txt/, readdir(DIR) );
@files = sort(@files);
closedir(DIR);

print "content-type:text/html\n\n <html>";
foreach $file(@files){
print "<li>$file";
}
print "</html>";
```

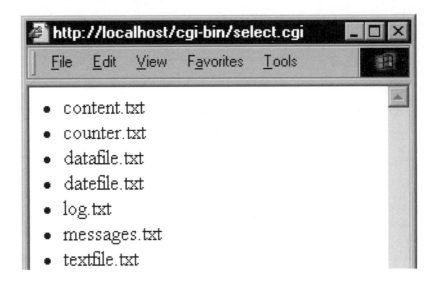

Create Directory

Perl can create new directories on the server using the "mkdir" function with two arguments.

For more on permissions see page 148.

The first argument specifies the name and address of the new directory folder.

The second argument sets the permissions code for the new directory that control how the folder can be accessed.

Typically the widest range of permissions are set with the code "0777" to permit read, write and execute operations.

The example below creates a new folder in the Xitami directory with these permissions:

```
#!C:/Perl/bin/perl

mkdir("../refs", 0777);
```

Delete Directory

Empty directories are removed with the "rmdir" function that takes a single argument to specify the directory address.

Attempts to delete a directory that is not empty will fail as seen in this example in which the "refs" directory contains a single file called "page.txt".

```
#!C:/Perl/bin/perl

rmdir("../refs")|| &error($!);

sub error{
print "content-type:text/html\n\n <html>";
print "Error: $_[0] </html>"; exit;
}
```

http://localhost/cgi-bin/deldir.cgi

File   Edit   View   Favorites   Tools

Error: Permission denied

To delete the directory the modified script below checks for the existence of the file called "page.txt" and removes it.

Now that the directory is empty it can also be deleted.

The special "-e" operator is used to check file status – See page 142.

```
#!C:/Perl/bin/perl

$file="../refs/page.txt";
if(-e $file){
unlink($file);
}

rmdir("../refs") || die &error($!);

sub error{
print "content-type:text/html\n\n <html>";
print "Error: $_[0] </html>";  exit;
}
```

Permission Values

Directories and files have an inherent set of permissions that control how they may be accessed for reading, writing and executing operations.

The permissions are given numeric values denoting if they can be read (4), write (2) and execute(1).

These may be combined by adding the numeric values. For instance, a file with read (4) and write (2) permissions, but not execute permission, would have a total value 6.

Permission values are given in this way to the three types of user who may access the directory or file in the strict order of "owner", "group" and "public".

The file's "owner" is generally the creator of the file who would always want at least read and write permissions.

The "group" permissions relate only to user groups on Unix systems so can usually be given the same permissions as those given to the "public" category.

Typically a directory would have generous permissions giving unlimited access to all three user types with a permissions value setting of 777.

In Perl the permissions code always requires a leading zero so the permissions code for this directory becomes 0777.

The table below lists commonly used permission settings showing how they affect each type of user with abbreviations of "r" for read, "w" for write and "x" for execute.

For setting permissions on the Unix server see page 181.

File Type	Permissions	Owner	Group	Public
Directory	0777	rwx	rwx	rwx
Executables eg. CGI scripts	0755	rwx	r-x	r-x
Non-executables eg. Text files	0644	rw-	r--	r--

Change Permissions

A script must have full directory permissions (7) to allow it to create, delete or rename files within that directory.

Permissions of directories and files can be changed by Perl scripts using the "chmod" function.

The "chmod" function takes two arguments to specify the permission code values and the address of the directory or file whose permissions are to be changed.

The example below tests for the existence of a directory before changing its permissions and writing a confirmation.

If the file is not found the alternative message is displayed.

If an error occurs the error-handling subroutine displays the error message to explain the problem.

Technically a directory that has been created from a Perl script has the script itself as its owner.

```perl
#!C:/Perl/bin/perl

print "content-type:text/html\n\n <html>";

if(-e "../refs"){
chmod(0777, "../refs") || &error($!);
print "Refs directory permissions set to 0777";
}else{
print "Refs directory was not found<br>";
print " - No permissions have changed."
}
print "</html>";

sub error{
print "Error: $_[0] </html>";
exit;
}
```

Change Working Directory

The "working" directory is normally the one containing the CGI script and is usually the cgi-bin directory on the server.

Other directories and files within the "working" directory can be addressed simply by their file name.

Directories and files outside the "working" directory must be referenced by their absolute or relative address.

The Perl "chdir" function can specify any directory as the "working" directory so its files can be addressed just by file name. This is convenient where a script uses several files contained in another directory.

This example makes a directory called "refs" into the "working" directory. You can then can address its files just by their names, without needing to state any path:

Single line statements may omit the final semi-colon and appear on one line of code as seen here.

```
#!C:/Perl/bin/perl

print "content-type:text/html\n\n <html>";

chdir("../refs") || &error($!);

if(-e "red.txt"){ print "<li>Local Red File Exists" }
if(-e "blue.txt"){ print "<li>Local Blue File Exists" }
print "</html>";

sub error{
print "Error: $_[0] </html>";
exit;
}
```

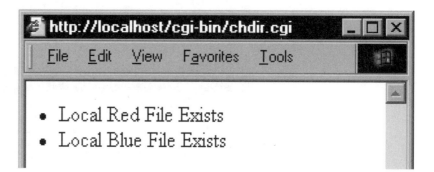

Data Persistence

This chapter illustrates how user data can be retained as the user browses across different web pages. There are demonstrations on how to store data in hidden forms, in server files and in browser cookies. Also examples demonstrate how access to cookie information is restricted.

Covers

Chapter Thirteen

Storing Data In Hidden Inputs

A Html form may contain hidden input fields that can be used to great effect by CGI scripts to store data.

A script that writes a Html document can include some hidden form inputs and assign stored data to their values.

In this way the hidden form inputs can retain stored data as the user moves from page to page.

The example illustrating this in action starts with a simple Html document containing a form with just two text inputs.

When the user submits this form to the server the CGI script extracts the entered values and assigns them to scalars.

The Html page created by this script writes these scalar values as hidden form values stored in the new Html form.

When the new Html form is submitted the next script extracts all form values including those in the hidden inputs.

Finally the script creates a Html document that displays the data entered by the user in both previous Html forms.

Keep the same name for data inputs to make the movement easier to follow.

```
<html>
<head><title>Order Items</title></head> <body>
<form method="post"
action="http://localhost/cgi-bin/order.cgi">
Item required: <input type="text" name="itm" size="15">
<br>Quantity: <input type="text" name="qty" size="3">
<input type="submit" value="Submit Items">
</form> </body> </html>
```

...cont'd

```
#!C:/Perl/bin/perl
require "formparser.lib"; &parseform;

print <<"DOC";
content-type:text/html\n\n <html>
<form action="http://localhost/cgi-bin/final.cgi"
method="post">
Name: <input type="text" name="name" size="15"><br>
City: <input type="text" name="city" size="10">
<input type="submit" value="Submit">
<input type="hidden" name="itm" value="$formdata{itm}">
<input type="hidden" name="qty" value="$formdata{qty}">
</form> </html>
DOC
```

This script adds an "s" to the end of the item for multiple-quantity orders.

```
#!C:/Perl/bin/perl
require "formparser.lib"; &parseform;
print "content-type:text/html\n\n";
print "<html><b>Thanks for your order...</b><br>";
print "$formdata{name} from $formdata{city}<br>";
print "has ordered $formdata{qty} $formdata{itm}";
if($formdata{qty} > 1){print "s"};
print "</html>";
```

Storing Data In Text Files

Data that has been entered by the user can be stored on the server in a text file so will not be lost as the user navigates around different pages.

The stored data can be retrieved for use in the generation of a new page at any time.

The following example is similar to the one on the previous page but now stores user input in a text file.

First the user enters data into a simple Html form:

```
<html>
<head><title>Order Items</title></head> <body>
<form method="post"
action="http://localhost/cgi-bin/order2.cgi">
Item required: <input type="text" name="itm" size="15">
<br> Quantity: <input type="text" name="qty" size="3">
<input type="submit" value="Submit Items">
</form> </body> </html>
```

The form values are then extracted and saved in a text file:

Add commas between saved data so they can be split into parts later.

```
#!C:/Perl/bin/perl
require "formparser.lib"; &parseform;

open(SAVE, ">save.txt");
print SAVE "$formdata{itm},$formdata{qty}";
close(SAVE);
print <<"DOC";
```

```
content-type:text/html\n\n <html>
<form action="http://localhost/cgi-bin/final2.cgi"
method="post">
Name: <input type="text" name="name" size="15"> <br>
City: <input type="text" name="city" size="10">
<input type="submit" value="Submit"> </form> </html>
DOC
```

```
http://localhost/cgi-bin/order2.cgi
File   Edit   View   Favorites   Tools
Name: Geoffrey
City: London        Submit
```

Finally the stored data is retrieved for display:

For more on reading text from files see page 132.

```
#!C:/Perl/bin/perl
require "formparser.lib"; &parseform;
open(SAVE, "<save.txt");
$list=<SAVE>;
close(SAVE);
@data=split( /,/ , $list);
print "content-type:text/html\n\n";
print "<html><b>Thanks for your order...</b><br>";
print "$formdata{name} from $formdata{city}<br>";
print "has ordered $data[1] $data[0]";
if($data[1] > 1){print "s"};
print "</html>";
```

```
http://localhost/cgi-bin/final2.cgi
File   Edit   View   Favorites   Tools

Thanks for your order...
Geoffrey from London
has ordered 3 Audio CDs
```

Internet Explorer Cookies

A cookie file can be used to store data on a user's computer in text format up to a limit of around 4000 characters.

The users computer can store up to 20 cookies from a single site and a maximum of 300 cookies in total.

On a Windows platform Internet Explorer saves the cookie files in a folder at C:\Windows\cookies.

The cookie file shown below contains two cookies that each start with the name and value of that cookie.

This is followed by the domain and path address of the document for which this cookie applies.

The list of numbers at the end of each cookie are just used by the local system to store the data.

This cookie file contains the cookies for the example on page 162.

📄 mike mcgrath@cgi-bin[2].txt

```
qtycookie
4
localhost/cgi-bin/
0
143147008
29609777
1853939584
29381346
*
itmcookie
Video DVD
localhost/cgi-bin/
0
143147008
29609777
1854539584
29381346
*
```

Netscape Cookies

On a Windows platform Netscape browsers store cookie data in a file called "cookies.txt" at C:\Netscape\Users in the current user's folder.

The cookies contain the domain and path details together with a numeric representation of the cookie expiry date. The cookie name and value is given at the end of each cookie.

The cookie file below shows the Netscape equivalent of the Internet Explorer cookie file on the opposite page:

For more on cookie expiry dates see the example on page 160.

```
📄 cookies.txt

# Netscape HTTP Cookie File

# http://www.netscape.com/newsref/
           std/cookie_spec.html

# This is a generated file!
  Do not edit.

localhost    FALSE    /cgi-bin
             FALSE    1072828800
             qtycookie    4

localhost    FALSE    /cgi-bin
             FALSE    1072828800
             itmcookie    Video DVD
```

Storing Data In Cookies

Form data can be stored in a cookie file so that another web page in that site can retrieve the data to use again.

Typically this creates a "shopping cart" arrangement where the user can add chosen items for totalling later.

Each item is added to the cookie file then all items can be finally retrieved for display on a summary page.

The first step is to send all the items data to the CGI script that will add the data to the cookie file.

The Html document shown below produces a form in which the user has entered data to add ten books to an order:

```html
<html>
<head>
<title>Order Items</title>
</head>
<body>

<form method="post"
action="http://localhost/cgi-bin/order4.cgi">

Item required: <input type="text" name="wot" size="15">
<br>
Quantity: <input type="text" name="num" size="3">
<input type="submit" value="Submit Items">
</form>
</body>
</html>
```

The submit button on the previous form sends the name/value pairs from the form to the CGI script shown below.

Each part of the submitted data is processed as normal by the form parser then each value is assigned to a new cookie.

Do not leave any space between the "Set-Cookie:" and the given name of the cookie.

Making a new cookie uses the syntax "Set-Cookie:" followed immediately by a given name to identify the data. The given names in the example are "wotcookie" and "numcookie".

Whenever a document cookie is set the environment variable called "$ENV{'HTTP_COOKIE'}" is set with all the cookie names and their associated values.

The contents of this variable appear in the Html output:

```perl
#!C:/Perl/bin/perl

require "formparser.lib"; &parseform;

print "Set-Cookie:wotcookie = $formdata{'wot'} \n";
print "Set-Cookie:numcookie = $formdata{'num'} \n";

print "content-type:text/html\n\n";
print "<html>";
print "<h3>Cookie Data:</h3>";
if($ENV{'HTTP_COOKIE'}){
print "$ENV{'HTTP_COOKIE'}";
}else{
print "No cookies set.";
}
print "</html>";
```

Note that this example will print a default message if no cookie is found.

Cookie Life Span

Unless an expiry date is specified when creating a cookie the life of the cookie is limited to the current browser session.

In this situation the cookie data is only stored in the computer RAM memory and a cookie file is not written. So when the browser application is terminated this transient cookie data is lost.

The cookie data is added to the cookies.txt file with Netscape. Otherwise the cookie is added to the folder at C:\Windows\cookies.

Setting an expiry date causes a cookie file to be written into the appropriate folder location. This means that the cookie data can be accessed over and over up to the expiry date.

To set an expiry date requires that the cookie's "expires" attribute be assigned a final date in a particular date format.

The date format should start with the 3-letter abbreviation for the weekday followed by a comma.

Next the date is stated in the format DD-MMM-YYYY where DD is a 2-digit day number of the month, MMM is a 3-letter abbreviation of a month and YYYY is a 4-digit year.

Then the time is stated in the format HH:MM:SS where HH is a 2-digit hour of a 24-hour clock, MM is a 2-digit number of minutes and SS is a 2-digit number of seconds.

Finally the time format is specified as Greenwich Mean Time using the abbreviation "GMT".

This example creates a cookie to expire at the end of 2003:

Re-setting the expiry date to a date before the present date will delete the cookie permanently.

```
#!C:/Perl/bin/perl
require "formparser.lib"; &parseform;
print "Set-Cookie:wotcookie = $formdata{'wot'};
expires=Wed,31-Dec-2003 00:00:00 GMT\n";
```

With Internet Explorer the new cookie may also be found among the cache in the Temporary Internet Files folder:

Internet Address	Expires
Cookie:mike mcgrath@localhost/cgi-bin/	31-12-2003 00:00

Restricting Access

When a cookie is created the current domain and path are assigned automatically to its "domain" and "path" attributes.

Only CGI scripts in that domain and on that path will be permitted to read the cookie data.

The cookie's " domain" attribute may only be assigned the domain from which the cookie is set to ensure that CGI scripts on other domains cannot access that cookie.

Access to the new cookie can be restricted to CGI scripts contained on a specific path by setting the "path" attribute.

Here a CGI script in the cgi-bin directory sets a cookie that can only be accessed by CGI scripts in the "cgi-bin/sub" sub-directory in the same domain:

```
#!C:/Perl/bin/perl
require "formparser.lib"; &parseform;

print "Set-Cookie:namecookie=$formdata{'name'};
expires=Wed,31-Dec-2003 00:00:00 GMT;
path=/cgi-bin/sub; \n";
```

Internet Address	Expires
Cookie:mike mcgrath@localhost/cgi-bin/sub	31-12-2003 00:00

CGI scripts in the "cgi-bin" directory cannot access the cookie created in this example.

The cookie could be set from a hyperlink such as http://localhost/cgi-bin/writecookie.cgi?name=CGI in easy steps.

Only CGI scripts in the sub-folder "cgi-bin/sub" can now access this cookie as illustrated below:

http://localhost/cgi-bin/sub/readcookie.cgi

File   Edit   View   Favorites   Tools   Help

Cookie value is CGI in easy steps

Using Cookie Data

Retrieving data from the cookie file requires that the pieces of cookie data must be split into their separate components.

The data in the cookie file is accessed via environment variable "$ENV{'HTTP_COOKIE'}".

Each cookie is automatically separated by a semi-colon and space when it was saved in the cookie file.

This can be used to split the cookies into an array where each element contains one name/value cookie pair.

Each of these pairs can then be split around the "=" into separate hashes to make the name/value data accessible.

This example first creates two cookies to store user input from an Html form then writes a second form:

The values from the example Html form inputs named "itm" and "qty" are stored in cookies named "itmcookie" and "qtycookie".

```
#!C:/Perl/bin/perl
require "formparser.lib"; &parseform;

print "Set-Cookie:itmcookie=$formdata{'itm'};
expires=Wed,31-Dec-2003 00:00:00 GMT\n";

print "Set-Cookie:qtycookie=$formdata{'qty'};
expires=Wed,31-Dec-2003 00:00:00 GMT\n";

print <<"DOC";
content-type:text/html\n\n <html>
<form action="http://localhost/cgi-bin/final3.cgi"
method="post">
Name: <input type="text" name="name" size="15"> <br>
City: <input type="text" name="city" size="10">
<input type="submit" value="Submit"> </form> </html>
DOC
```

When the second form is submitted the CGI script below splits the cookies into an array called "@cookies" then splits each pair into a hash called "%data".

The script finally writes a Html page that uses both the data retrieved from the cookies and the second form input:

The original Html form input values are now accessible from the "%data" hash by specifying the cookie name as the key.

```perl
#!C:/Perl/bin/perl

require "formparser.lib"; &parseform;

if($ENV{'HTTP_COOKIE'}){
@cookies=split(/; /,$ENV{'HTTP_COOKIE'});
foreach $cookie(@cookies){
($name, $value)=split(/=/, $cookie);
$data{$name}=$value; }
}

print "content-type:text/html\n\n";
print "<html><b>Thanks for your order...</b><br>";
print "$formdata{name} from $formdata{city}<br>";
print "ordered $data{'qtycookie'} $data{'itmcookie'}";
if($data{'qtycookie'} > 1){print "s"};
print "</html>";
```

Refused Cookie Message

If the user has selected browser settings to disallow cookies it is worthwhile providing a message to explain that the cookie data required by a script cannot be found.

The example below adds an alternative subroutine to the script on the previous page that will write a message if the "$ENV{'HTTP_COOKIE'}" variable is empty.

It is very safe to allow cookies on a computer but some users are still wary.

```
#!C:/Perl/bin/perl
require "formparser.lib"; &parseform;

if($ENV{'HTTP_COOKIE'}){
@cookies=split(/; /,$ENV{'HTTP_COOKIE'});
foreach $cookie(@cookies){
($name, $value)=split(/=/, $cookie);
$data{$name}=$value; }
}else{ &notice; }

print "content-type:text/html\n\n";
print "<html><b>Thanks for your order...</b><br>";
print "$formdata{name} from $formdata{city}<br>";
print "ordered $data{'qtycookie'} $data{'itmcookie'}";
if($data{'qtycookie'} > 1){print "s"};
print "</html>";

sub notice{
print "content-type:text/html\n\n <html>";
print "<b>The browser cannot find required data</b>";
print "<br>Please ensure";
print "<br>that your browser settings allow cookies";
print "</html>";
exit; }
```

Form Inputs

This chapter demonstrates how Perl CGI scripts can use different types of Html form input from check boxes, radio buttons, and options menus. Also examples show how Perl can navigate between web pages and send email. Lastly a survey application illustrates some of these features in use.

Covers

Chapter Fourteen

Check Boxes

Check boxes are used to allow users to select items in a Html form. Each check box must have a unique name assigned to its "name" attribute in the Html code.

Also each check box "value" attribute should be assigned a value to be associated with that box.

The following example illustrates a Html form containing a list of check boxes.

When the form is submitted the name/value pairs of any selected check boxes are processed by the form parser. All the selected values are then displayed in the Html output.

When a form is submitted only the name/value pair of any selected check boxes will be sent to the server.

```
<html> <head> <title>Check Boxes</title> </head> <body>

<form name="f" method="post"
action="http://localhost/cgi-bin/chkbox.cgi">

<b>Select 3 Favourite Destinations: </b> <br>
<input type="checkbox" name="NY" value="New York">
New York <br>
<input type="checkbox" name="SF" value="San Francisco">
San Francisco <br>
<input type="checkbox" name="TY" value="Tokyo">
Tokyo <br>
<input type="checkbox" name="SY" value="Sydney">
Sydney <br>
<input type="checkbox" name="CA" value="Cape Town">
Cape Town <br>
<input type="checkbox" name="AT" value="Athens">
Athens <br>
<input type="checkbox" name="MO" value="Moscow">
Moscow <br>
<input type="checkbox" name="PA" value="Paris">
Paris <br>
<input type="checkbox" name="LO" value="London">
London <br>
<input type="submit" value="Submit Selections">

</form>
</body> </html>
```

...cont'd

```
#!C:/Perl/bin/perl
require "formparser.lib"; &parseform;
print "Content-type: text/html\n\n <html>";
print "<h3>Favourite Destinations Selected:</h3>";
foreach $key (keys %formdata){print
"<li>$formdata{$key}";}
print "</html>";
```

Radio Buttons

Radio button inputs are named after the type of real buttons used on old radios that allowed selection of a pre-set station.

Pushing one button de-selected the previous selection so only one station could be selected at any given time.

In Html, radio button inputs work in just the same way – allowing only one input to be selected at any given time.

Radio buttons are grouped together by setting their "name" attribute to a common name. That group will then only allow a single button within the group to ever be selected.

Each of the radio buttons in a group have individual values assigned to their "value" attributes that makes them unique.

When a form is submitted it is the name/value pair of the selected radio button in the group that is sent to the server.

The following example illustrates a Html document containing a form with two groups of radio buttons:

Always use meaningful names for the radio button groups.

```
<html>
<head><title>Radio Button Groups</title></head>
<body>

<form name="f" method="post"
action="http://localhost/cgi-bin/radio.cgi">
<b>Select a colour: </b>
<input type="radio" name="Colour" value="Red"> Red
<input type="radio" name="Colour" value="Green"> Green
<input type="radio" name="Colour" value="Blue"> Blue
<br>
<b>Select a number: </b>
<input type="radio" name="Number" value="One"> One
<input type="radio" name="Number" value="Two"> Two
<input type="radio" name="Number" value="Three"> Three
<p>
<input type="submit" value="Submit Selections">
</form>
</body>
</html>
```

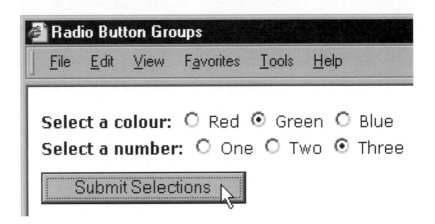

The submitted name/value pairs are processed by the form parser and each component is displayed by the Html output.

```
#!C:/Perl/bin/perl

require "formparser.lib";
&parseform;

print "Content-type: text/html\n\n";
print "<html>";
print "<h3>Radio Button Selections:</h3>"
foreach $key (keys %formdata){
print "<li>$key selected is $formdata{$key}";
}
print "</html>";
```

Option Menus

The options menus enclosed by the Html "select" tags allow the user to choose an item from a menu list.

A name/value pair sent to the server from an options menu is drawn from separate Html tags.

The name component is that of the "name" attribute specified in the Html "select" tag.

The "value" component is the value of the option that is selected when the form is submitted.

This example creates two options menus with name components of "day" and "month":

Omit the size attributes from the "select" tags to have the options display "drop-down" menus.

```
<html>
<head><title>Option Menus</title>
</head>
<body>

<form name="f" method="post"
action="http://localhost/cgi-bin/menus.cgi">
<b>Select A Date: </b><br>

<select name="day" size="5">
<option value="18th">18
<option value="19th">19
<option value="20th">20
<option value="21st">21
<option value="22nd">22
</select>

<select name="month" size="5">
<option value="January">Jan
<option value="February">Feb
<option value="March">Mar
<option value="April">Apr
<option value="May">May
</select>

<input type="submit" value="Submit Date">

</form> </body> </html>
```

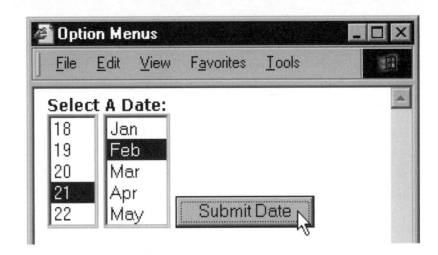

The name/value pairs that are submitted by the form are processed by the form parser in the usual way.

Each value can be addressed in the "%formdata" hash using the name assigned to the select tag's "name" attribute.

The values are then displayed in the Html output.

Notice that the actual values are verbose versions of the menu items.

```
#!C:/Perl/bin/perl

require "formparser.lib";
&parseform;

print "Content-type: text/html\n\n";
print "<html>";
print "<b>Selected Date: </b>";
print "$formdata{'day'} $formdata{'month'}";
print "</html>";
```

All inputs (text, textarea, checkbox, radio and option menus) provide a means for the user to create a name/value pair.

Redirect

Perl can be used to redirect a web browser to a Html page containing content specifically written for just that browser.

The method to achieve this employs the "Location:" header.

For about the "Content-type:" header and "MIME" types see page 18.

This header is used in place of the usual "Content-type:" header that specifies the MIME type.

The "Location:" header instead specifies the URL to which the browser should be redirected.

In this example the browser identity string is assigned to a scalar which is then searched to match individual browsers.

The browser will load a page containing content appropriate for either Internet Explorer, Netscape or other browsers.

```
#!C:/Perl/bin/perl

$browser=$ENV{'HTTP_USER_AGENT'};

if( $browser =~ m/MSIE/i ){
print "Location: http://localhost/ie_page.html";
}

elsif( $browser =~ m/Mozilla/i ){
print "Location: http://localhost/nn_page.html";
}

else{
print "Location: http://localhost/other.html";
}
```

For more about matching string patterns see page 102.

If the web browser is Internet Explorer this page will load:

If the web browser is Netscape Navigator this page will load:

Other browsers will load this default page:

Here the Opera web browser uses its own identity but it can optionally be set to identify itself like Netscape Navigator or Microsoft Internet Explorer.

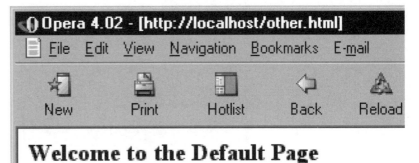

Mail Response

A Perl CGI script can send an automatic response by email if the server has an email program available.

Mostly Unix web servers have a program called "sendmail" for this purpose although its directory location can change.

Accessing the "sendmail" program from a Perl script is similar to the way that text files are read and written.

The program must first be opened and a file handle label given. A "|" pipe character should immediately precede the "sendmail" location to indicate that it is a program.

Once opened the "print" function can write the email data then the "close" function must finally close the text stream.

The example illustrates a CGI script located on a Unix server with the Perl interpreter in the "usr/bin" directory and the "sendmail" program in the "usr/lib" directory.

After the email data is sent to "sendmail" the script will write a Html message for the user.

This Html form submits data to the CGI script from a text input named "adr" and from a text area named "msg".

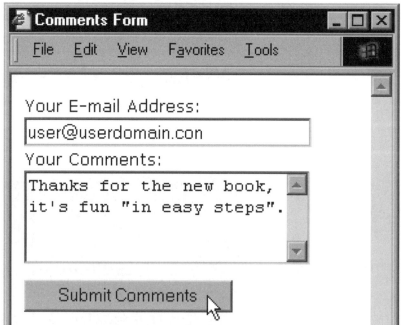

...cont'd

The " -t" switch instructs the "sendmail" program to look for incoming data for "To:", "From:" and "Subject:" message lines.

```perl
#!/usr/bin/perl
require "formparser.lib"; &parseform;
$adr = $formdata{'adr'};
$msg = $formdata{'msg'};

open(REPLY, "|/usr/lib/sendmail -t");
print REPLY "To: $adr \n";
print REPLY "From: sender\@serverdomain.com \n";
print REPLY "Subject: Your Comments \n";
print REPLY "This information was submitted:\n";
print REPLY "$msg Your comments are appreciated.";
close REPLY;

print "Content-type: text/html\n\n <html>";
print "<b>Thanks for your input!</b><br>";
if ($adr && $msg) {
print "You should get an autoresponse soon.<p>";}
print "Please click back. </html>";
```

Always escape special script characters – like the "@" in an email address.

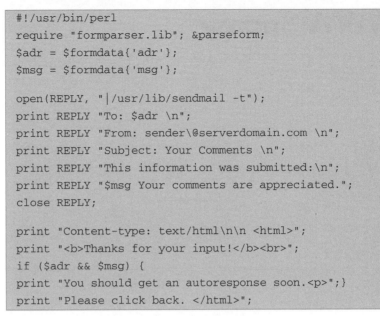

WWW Survey

The code below creates a Html document consisting of a single survey form that can be submitted to a CGI script.

This form contains an example of each type of form input.

This code has been somewhat compacted to fit it within the available space.

```html
<html><head><title>WWW Survey</title></head>
<body bgcolor="black">
<form action="http://localhost/cgi-bin/poll.cgi">
<table border="1" bgcolor="white" width="100%">
<tr><td>   <b>Please select your browser:</b> <br>
<input type="radio" name="browser"
value="Internet Explorer">  Internet Explorer<br>
<input type="radio" name="browser"
value="Netscape Navigator"> Netscape Navigator<br>
<input type="radio" name="browser"
value="a minor browser">  Other<br>
</td></tr><tr><td>
<b>Where do you access the web ?</b>  <br>
<input type="checkbox" name="home" value="at home">
At home<br>
<input type="checkbox" name="work" value="at work">
At the office<br>
<input type="checkbox" name="move" value="on the move">
While travelling<br>
</td></tr><tr><td>   <b>On which platform ?</b>
<select name="platform">
<option value="Microsoft Windows" selected> Windows
<option value="Unix/Linux"> Unix/Linux
<option value="a minor platform"> Other
</select>
</td></tr><tr><td><b>How could the web be improved ?</b>
<textarea rows="3" cols="28" name="comments"></textarea>
</td></tr><tr><td>
<b>Please enter your e-mail address:</b>
<input type="text" size="32" name="user">
</td></tr><tr><td>
<input type="submit" value="Click Here To Submit Form">
</td></tr></table>
</form>
</body></html>
```

WWW Survey

File   Edit   View   Favorites   Tools

Please select your browser:
- ⦿ Internet Explorer
- ○ Netscape Navigator
- ○ Other

Where do you access the web ?
- ☑ At home
- ☑ At the office
- ☐ While travelling

On which platform ?   Windows ▾

How could the web be improved ?

Increase bandwidth.
Remove offensive content.

Please enter your e-mail address:

user@userdomain.com

Click Here To Submit Form

HOT TIP

Checks could be added to see that all form fields are "required" so that the user cannot submit a partially completed form.

The survey form is shown above with selected user entries.

When the user pushes the submit button all the form data is sent to the script detailed overleaf.

The form parser separates all the name/value pairs so that the script can use their values to write a Html response page.

Individual tests are made to see if the value exists before writing a descriptive line of text about that entry.

```
#!C:/Perl/bin/perl
require "formparser.lib"; &parseform;

print "Content-type: text/html\n\n <html>";
print "<title>Survey Data Received</title>";
print "The following information was received:<p>";
if($formdata{'user'}){
print "<li>From: $formdata{'user'}";}
if($formdata{'browser'}){
print "<li>Browser in use is $formdata{'browser'}";}
if($formdata{'home'}){
print "<li>Web access is available $formdata{'home'}";}
if($formdata{'work'}){
print "<li>Web access is available $formdata{'work'}";}
if($formdata{'move'}){
print "<li>Web access is available $formdata{'move'}";}
if($formdata{'platform'}){
print "<li>Platform used is $formdata{'platform'}";}
if($formdata{'idea'}){
print "<li>Suggested improvement:<p>$formdata{'idea'}";}
print "<p>Thank you for participating.</html>";
```

Remember to thank users for taking part in this kind of survey.

Survey Data Received

File   Edit   View   Favorites   Tools

The following information was received:

- From: user@userdomain.com
- Browser in use is Internet Explorer
- Web access is available at home
- Web access is available at work
- Platform used is Microsoft Windows
- Suggested improvement:

Increase bandwidth. Remove offensive content.

Thank you for participating.

Upload & Run Scripts

This final chapter demonstrates how to upload Perl CGI scripts to a web server so that the scripts will perform correctly. Also examples illustrate how scripts can be restricted to run only from origins on the same server. Using third-party scripts and libraries is explained with addresses where CGI resources can be obtained for free.

Covers

Chapter Fifteen

FTP Upload

Running CGI scripts on the internet normally requires that the files are uploaded to an Internet Service Provider (ISP).

The ISP will advise where CGI scripts can be located on their server and of any restrictions that they may impose.

It is most convenient to upload files by File Transfer Protocol (FTP) using an FTP Client program.

Most ISP servers run a Unix operating system but using an FTP Client means that no knowledge of Unix is needed.

The world's leading FTP client is Cute FTP from GlobalSCAPE Inc. and is available for download from their web site at http://www.cuteftp.com.

Some ISPs do not allow CGI scripts – but it's easy to change to another ISP.

/cgi-bin		
Name	Size	Attr
sub	512	drwxr-xr-x
formparser.lib	894	-rw-r—r—
hello.cgi	101	-rwxr-xr-x

The CGI location directory may often be the cgi-bin directory on the ISP server in the same way that the Xitami examples have been using the C:\Xitami\cgi-bin directory.

It is important to know the location of the Perl interpreter on the ISP server as the shebang line in each CGI script needs to be amended accordingly before it is uploaded.

The shebang line must correctly state the server location of Perl if the script is to run properly from the sever.

To avoid possible problems when loaded on the server the FTP Client options should always be set to upload CGI scripts as ASCII or text files – not as binary files.

Setting Permissions

When CGI script files have been uploaded to the ISP's server their file permissions need to be set to restrict how the files may be used.

Permissions are depicted in the "Attr" column in the illustration on the facing page that shows a sub-directory, a library file and a CGI script file.

The permissions can be set after uploading the files from the FTP Client using the "chmod" facility to specify the permissions for owner, group and public access.

Owners will always want full permissions but other groups should be denied the permission to write to the files. Library files are not executable so do not need that permission.

 The numeric value for permissions are an addition for each group where read=4, write=2 and executable=1. Normally set files and directories to 755 and library files to 644.

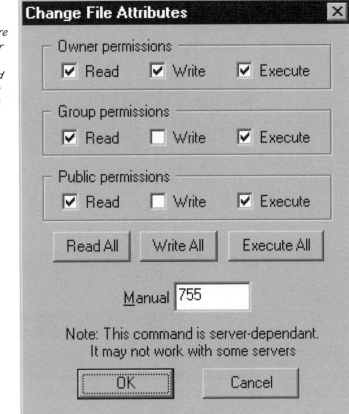

HTTP Referer

The environment variable "$ENV{'HTTP_REFERER'}" contains the Url of the web page last visited before the CGI script was run.

If the script is run from a Html document containing a link then the "$ENV{'HTTP_REFERER'}" variable is set with the Url of the page that contains the link.

This can be useful to gauge where traffic to a web site is originating although it is not wholly accurate as the variable may have been set in a different manner.

Notice that the spelling of the variable name does not have four "Rs" so is not "HTTP_REFERRER".

For instance, when a script is run by typing its address into the browser's address bar the "$ENV{'HTTP_REFERER'}" is set with whatever page was last visited by the browser. This happens irrespective of whether that page contains a link to the CGI script.

This example shows a Html page containing a link to a CGI script displaying the "$ENV{'HTTP_REFERER'}" variable.

```
#!C:/Perl/bin/perl
print "Content-type: text/html\n\n <html>";
print "Originator: $ENV{'HTTP_REFERER'} </html>";
```

Restricted Running

The example on the facing page demonstrates that the "$ENV{'HTTP_REFERER'}$" variable will be set to the Url of the page containing a link to a CGI script.

To ensure that CGI scripts are only run from pages on the same server this variable can be tested.

The example below checks that the link is contained in a page on the "localhost" server before permitting the script to run or will display an alternate message:

```perl
#!C:/Perl/bin/perl

$start=$ENV{'HTTP_REFERER'};
$this_server="http://localhost/";
print "Content-type: text/html\n\n <html>";
if( $start =~ m/$this_server/i ){
print "<b>OK:</b><br>";
print "CGI script is accessed from this server.";
}else{
print "<b>Unauthorized Access:</b><br>";
print "CGI script cannot run from that location!";
}
print "</html>";
```

This top example output was run from the "localhost" domain. The bottom example output was run from another domain.

Ready-Made Scripts & Libraries

Lots of ready-made CGI Perl scripts are freely available on the internet. It is often worthwhile checking to see if a script already exists that can be tailored to meet your needs.

The top three sources recommended by this book to search for ready-made CGI Perl scripts are listed below:

1

The most comprehensive web site for CGI with hundreds of scripts, articles and masses of related information at http://www.cgi-resources.com.

2

A wealth of scripts in a wide variety of scripting languages including Perl CGI scripts. The lists are broken down into categories that make it easy to find what you need at http://www.scriptsearch.com.

3

Matt Wright provides one of the most popular web sites to find useful free CGI scripts in "Matt's Script Archive". This is often referred to as simply "MSA" and is located at http://www.msa.com/scripts.

Configuring Ready-Made Scripts

When a suitable ready-made script has been located it will be necessary to configure it to suit its new purpose.

Usually the author will have provided instructions in the source code to help determine what needs to be changed.

Sometimes the author will have placed all the configurable components in a separate configuration file.

It is good practice to make a back-up copy of the script and all files provided with the script. This provides a quick and easy way to review the original code if needed.

The first step in configuration is to read the author's notes.

If the script source code contains a copyright notice any restrictions that may have been placed on how the script may be used should be observed.

Ensure that the shebang line is set to the location of the Perl interpreter on the server that will run the script.

Similarly, change the path addresses of files and directories to suit the server that will be running the script.

Amend any variable values within the script so that they are appropriate to its new purpose.

The output Html code will normally need to be changed to suit the new use of the script. Edit the source code to create the appropriate Html output.

Using the information and examples contained in this book the script may be further customized until it completely fulfils the precise requirements of its new role.

As with all scripts it should be tested thoroughly in as many ways as possible before it is uploaded to the server.

The author may like to learn of any useful additions or amendments that have been made to the original script.

It is always courteous to send an email to the author to say a "Thank You" for providing a free script resource.

More Perl Resources

This book will, hopefully, have provided you with a great introduction to the use of Perl in CGI scripts and may have whetted your appetite to find out even more.

The first place to look is the comprehensive Perl documentation that accompanies the Perl interpreter in the download package from Active State.

The documentation includes much more detail on Perl for use in CGI and other applications.

www.perl.com

To learn of the latest Perl developments, and much more, the Perl web site is essential viewing.

In addition to Perl news all versions of the Perl interpreter are available from here in both source code and binary version for a variety of operating systems.

Perl documentation can also be downloaded from this site.

There is a very useful Frequently Asked Questions (FAQ) section and a searchable Reference section that can prove immensely helpful when developing Perl skills.

Feature articles on Perl provide interesting reading too and the site has links to many Perl tutorials and training courses.

Visitors can subscribe to "The Perl Journal" quarterly magazine to keep regularly posted about new Perl events.

Details of forthcoming Perl conferences are posted and there is a selection of programming tools for download.

Lastly, the site provides a link to the Comprehensive Perl Archive Network (CPAN) which is mirrored at over 100 sites. This aims to provide all the Perl material you will ever need and contains literally hundreds of megabytes of data.

This rich supply of information provides many avenues to explore if you wish to build upon the knowledge you have gained from "CGI & Perl in easy steps" – happy scripting!

Index